HOW TO

Stay

Sane

WHEN LIFE DOESN'T MAKE SENSE

J.O. and Juanita Purcell

REGULAR BAPTIST PRESS
1300 North Meacham Road
Schaumburg, Illinois 60173-4806

HOW TO STAY SANE WHEN LIFE DOESN'T MAKE SENSE
© 1999
Regular Baptist Press • Schaumburg, Illinois
1-800-727-4440 • www.regularbaptistpress.org
Printed in U.S.A.
All rights reserved
RBP5241 • ISBN: 0-87227-199-4
Second printing—2003

Dedication

TO OUR DEAR FRIENDS at Heritage Baptist Church in Lakeland, Florida, who allowed us the privilege of ministering to them for eighteen years. The joyful times and the painful times enriched our lives and equipped us to be better servants. These experiences taught us the lessons we are teaching in this book. Our desire is to enrich other lives so they may know the values of encouragement, rebuke, empathy, and forgiveness.

Contents

PART ONE

God Always Does What Is Right— Even When It Doesn't Seem Right!

PART TWO

Questions We Ask When Life Doesn't Make Sense

Preface

WHY, GOD? This question, more than any other, plagues Christians and makes sleepless nights seem like an eternity. When we are not delivered from our adversities, we wonder why. Didn't God deliver David? "This poor man cried, and the LORD heard him, and saved him out of all his troubles" (Psalm 34:6). When we pray for a miracle but don't get one, we wonder why. Didn't God say, "For verily I say unto you, That whosoever shall say unto this mountain, Be thou removed, and be thou cast into the sea; and shall not doubt in his heart, but shall believe that those things which he saith shall come to pass; he shall have whatsoever he saith" (Mark 11:23)? What happened? Did we fail to have enough faith, or did God fail us?

Why? Why? Why? We know God's Word is true. And we know that God never fails, but sometimes life just doesn't make much sense to us. We want everything to make sense; we want logical answers to our questions. Would we bear our trials any better or would the suffering seem less intense if we knew why? Probably not! If we knew why, could we keep something bad from happening? Probably not!

"Why?" is not really a good question, because it doesn't solve anything. Instead of asking why, we would be wiser to ask how. *How* can I trust God more so I can ask why less? When I can't understand the "why's" of life, I can still know the "Who" of life. As Charles Spurgeon once said, "When you can't trace God's hand, trust His heart."

Trusting is often harder than obeying. With obeying, we have had the boundaries of obedience explained to us, but trusting God has no explained boundaries—we are always dealing with the unknown. We don't know what trials we will have to endure, how

7

long a trial will continue, or how frequently we must endure our trials. To trust God, we must come to the place where we can see our adverse circumstances through eyes of faith, not of sense.

Our purpose in writing these lessons is to encourage you to trust God when life doesn't make sense. We have learned by experience that trusting God works!

Part 1

God Always Does What Is Right—
Even When It Doesn't
Seem Right!

Lord, Why Is This Happening?

WHEN adversities charge into our lives, we often ask why. "Why me and not the alcoholic who can't keep a job?" "Why me and not the guy down the street who beats his wife and kids?" "Why me and not the woman who steps out on her husband?" It is natural to ask why when our lives seem to be topsy-turvy. Even our Savior asked why when He agonized on the cross as He died for our sins: "My God, my God, why hast thou forsaken me?" (Matthew 27:46; emphasis added). We all ask why. The problem is that our questioning spirit becomes demanding. We demand because we were born with a sinful, selfish nature.

We demand our children to respond correctly—after all, look what we have done for them! We demand that our mate meet our needs—isn't that what God commands? We demand people move as soon as the light turns green—we don't have all day to wait on slow people. If we are not careful, we will find ourselves demanding God, Who created us, to respond to our orders as well.

1. What orders do people shout to God?

2. How foolish it is to shout orders to a sovereign God. What

does the statement "God is sovereign" mean to you? Read Psalm 135:6.

From MY Perspective—J. O.

Isn't it amazing? God is not subject to the plans that we make. Never once does He ask us, "Would you like to have cancer? lose your child in death? be terminated from your job?" No, He just allows these things for His own purpose as part of His plan for our lives. The things God allows will make us more demanding, critical, and bitter or make us better, sweeter, and less insistent on answers from God. We must never forget that God is in control! He gives the orders—not us. He orders our steps and our stops. "The steps of a good man are ordered by the LORD" (Psalm 37:23).

3. Have you ever felt God uniquely designed a difficult circumstance for your life just to frustrate you? What was it?

4. Look at Exodus 13:21 and Numbers 9:15–23. Our sovereign God guided the Children of Israel through the wilderness with a cloud by day and a pillar of fire at night. How could this experience have been frustrating for two million or more people traveling together?

From MY Perspective—Juanita

Try to imagine what it might have been like traveling—on foot—with your family and two million or more companions in the wilderness. You're tired, your husband is complaining, the kids are crying and whining. You keep thinking, "When is that pillar of fire going to stop moving?" But as time goes on, you seem to be revived; you can make it for a few more hours. Just when you are set to keep going, the pillar of fire stops; and you think, "Why now?" All the people stop, unload, and set up their tents. Just as everyone dozes off for a much-needed night's rest, the pillar of fire starts moving. Everyone must pack and move again. And you ask, "Why, God?"

Do you ever feel as if God is trying to frustrate you? He could stop things from happening, but He doesn't. Does God do things just to frustrate us? NO! However, we need to deal with our frustration with God. Frustration can plant in our hearts seeds that may develop into a habitual attitude of questioning God's fairness. Is He unfair in the way He is treating us? No!

We all question God now and then, but we must be careful that we don't develop a questioning spirit that wants answers to the "why's."

5. Read Job 10:1 and 2. What Bible character developed a questioning spirit with God?

We remember Job as a patient man, and he was: "Ye have heard of the patience of Job" (James 5:11). However, even his patience ran out, and he started wanting some answers from God. Let's look at Job's struggles with his trial. He moved from acceptance to a questioning spirit and back to acceptance.

6. What did Job lose? See Job 1:13–19.

7. Describe Job's attitude. Read Job 1:21.

8. Job lost his cattle, his servants, and his children. What other trial did God allow into his life? See Job 2:7.

From MY Perspective—J. O.

I once read of two young men who experienced great tragedies in their lives. One went on to live a happy, successful life; but the other ended in bitterness. What made the difference? One word—acceptance!

Worral had been stricken with rheumatoid arthritis at age fifteen. By age forty-five he was totally paralyzed (except for one finger) and totally blind. He tied a string to his one mobile finger so that he could turn on a recorder. From his bed, he led a happy, productive life writing for national magazines and writing books. God had not answered his prayer for healing, so he graciously accepted his lot in life and said, "Well, Lord! If this is the size plot you've stacked out for me, let's You and me together show the world what we can grow on it."

Cliff, a powerfully built construction worker, fell from a dirt-moving machine and sheared his spinal cord at the age of eighteen. He was told he would never sit or walk again. Cliff insisted, "God never intended anyone to live like this." He used all his energies and efforts expecting a miracle, but no healing ever came. Cliff became a critical, bitter man as he wasted his life demanding God to heal him.

What a difference acceptance brings into our lives. In acceptance there is peace. Oh, how long it takes some of us to learn that lesson!

9. What was Job's attitude after Satan sent the boils (Job 2:7)? Read verse 10.

10. Job had three friends who came to give him counsel on how to handle his problems. What were their thoughts about God? Read Job 8:5–7.

11. What did they encourage Job to do?

12. What was Job's response? Read Job 9:1–4, 14, and 15.

In Job 9:16 we see Job's confidence beginning to weaken. Job began to paint an incorrect picture of God. He stated that God afflicts for no reason (v. 17), overwhelms people with all kinds of misery (v. 18), laughs at the pain of the innocent (v. 23), and allows injustice (v. 24).

13. What two words addressed to God in Job 10:2 expose the beginning of a questioning spirit?

From MY Perspective—Juanita

We have all been where Job was, haven't we? When we pray and pray and nothing happens, it is easy for our confidence to weaken. Whether we realize it or not, it is easy for a questioning spirit to develop when nothing happens and we know God could change things if He would. The longer our misery continues, the more unfair everything seems. We might even begin to feel God hates us. When we feel this questioning spirit begin to develop, we need to see it as an alarm and start spending less time looking for answers from God and more time thinking about the attributes of God. God is just, loving, kind, patient, faithful, and compassionate.

Why not get out a piece of paper and list an attribute of God for each letter of the alphabet.

Here is a promise and a challenge: "Thou wilt keep him in perfect peace, whose mind is stayed on thee: because he trusteth in thee. Trust ye in the LORD for ever: for in the LORD JEHOVAH is everlasting strength" (Isaiah 26:3, 4). Keeping your mind stayed on Christ will allow you to change your focus. Instead of dwelling on your problems, focus on your powerful God.

14. When we demand answers and relief but nothing changes, it is easy to develop a "poor me" spirit. What did Job call his three friends? Read Job 16:2.

15. How did he feel about God? Read Job 16:7–9.

16. Read Job 19:7. What words in this verse indicate Job had developed a "poor me" spirit?

17. In Job 23:1–7 we see Job's questioning spirit at full bloom. What words in verse 5 indicate that he was demanding some answers?

18. When pain goes on and on, we often try to persuade God how reasonable it is to do things our way. Why do we tend to measure other people's love for us by the way they agree with our plans?

19. Why is this behavior childish?

From MY Perspective—J. O.

Job 23:10–17 is a beautiful interlude in the midst of Job's struggles. Verses 10 and 14 give us reason to believe that Job was remembering again how great God is. Job was coming to grips with the fact that God could still see him, even if he could not see God. "But he knoweth the way that I take: when he hath tried me, I shall come forth as gold" (v. 10); "for he performeth the thing that is appointed for me" (v. 14). Job seemed to be acknowledging the fact that his trials were a testing that God had appointed for his life. Job realized God could not be controlled by his cries for answers and that God might not give him answers.

When we finally realize God may not do what we ask, we have made progress. God does not always make everything right—from our perspective. From His perspective, His actions are always right: "As for God, his way is perfect" (Psalm 18:30).

20. Job kept wanting an audience with God. Finally God spoke to Job, as recorded in Job 38. However, God did not answer any of Job's questions. He told Job to brace himself because He was going to ask him some questions. What are some of the questions God asked Job?

Job 38:4, 5—

Job 38:12—

Job 40:2—

Job 40:8—

21. How would you summarize the lesson God wanted to teach Job with all His questions?

22. How did Job respond? See Job 42:1–6.

From MY Perspective—Juanita

Sixteen times Job had hurled his "why's" to God. Never once did God answer the question why. Fifty-nine times we see the word "why" in reference to God. Job did not need to know why. He needed to know who; Who was in control! When Job changed the *y* to an *o*, he finally found relief. His preoccupation with why changed to a submission and trust in Who when he had a personal encounter with God. "Now mine eye seeth thee" (Job 42:5). Job moved from acceptance to demanding answers and then back to acceptance.

When we, like Job, finally see God in our circumstances, we will also see ourselves differently. We will see ourselves as vessels whom God is trying to shape for His honor and glory. We will also come to realize that He wants us to love and trust Him and not necessarily because of what He does or does not give us. He wants us to love Him because of Who He is—our almighty, awesome, all-loving God.

We don't need to know why; He knows why. Knowing that I am not in total control of my life takes the pressure off me and puts it on God—He is in control. Personally knowing the One Who is in charge of every detail of my life brings great relief and confidence. We must pray much, desire much, plan much, and expect much—but demand nothing! God is God and owes us no answers.

From YOUR Perspective

Have you had a questioning spirit—even a demanding spirit? Have you been asking God to let you see how a situation is going to end or to let you see why it is happening? Will you let go of your questions? Will you quit trying to find answers? If so, will you pray this prayer with us?

> *Lord, forgive me for not trusting You; forgive me for demanding answers. Right now I turn loose my questioning spirit—it is enough for me to know that You are in control and nothing touches my life that does not first pass through Your loving hand. I accept Your appointment for my life and believe the truths in Psalm 18:30, even though I don't understand the situation right now.*

"As for God, his way is perfect" (2 Samuel 22:31).

Can God Really Be in Everything?

WHY are we, like Job, so slow to realize that our sovereign God is in absolute control of us and of this world that He created? Often we are slow to admit that He always does what is right. And He does always do what is right: "Shall not the Judge of all the earth do right?" (Genesis 18:25). We know academically that God is in control, but we seem to forget this fact when everything appears to be going wrong. Our minds are confused, and it seems to us that God is not aware of our need. We cry out, "Where are You, God, when I need You?"

We may forget it, or we may not believe it, but it is true—God is sovereign! He does what He plans, and He determines whether we may or may not do what we have planned. No one can thwart His will or act outside the bounds of His will. God is on His throne ruling this universe according to His sovereign will and good pleasure. Not even a sparrow falls to the ground or a hair falls from someone's head that God does not see. How comforting it is to know that our God is so intimately involved in each of our lives.

In this lesson we desire to help you come to the place where you can see God in everything and trust His sovereign care and control.

Nothing Touches Our Lives That God Does Not Allow
1. Read Lamentations 3:37. What does this verse teach us about God's sovereign control?

2. James 4:15 states that when we make our plans for the future, we "ought to say, If the Lord will, we shall live, and do this, or that." How does this verse relate to Proverbs 16:9?

3. How would Proverbs 19:21 encourage your heart if someone told you that he would destroy you in one way or another?

From MY Perspective—Juanita

Many years ago I read a statement by an old saint of God that has helped me so much to see God in everything.

> *It may be the sin of man that originates the action, and therefore the thing itself cannot be said to be the will of God; but by the time it reaches us it has become God's will for us, and must be accepted as directly from His hands. No man or company of men, no power in earth or heaven, can touch that soul which is abiding in Christ, without first passing through His encircling presence, and receiving the seal of His permission.*[1]

I think 1 Thessalonians 5:18 states her thoughts in one short verse: "In every thing give thanks: for this is the will of God in Christ Jesus concerning you."

God knows those "if need be's" that are necessary in my life: "Wherein ye greatly rejoice, though now for a season, *if need be,* ye are in heaviness through manifold temptations" (1 Peter 1:6; emphasis added). The "need be's" seldom make much sense to me when I am in the midst of the trial, but knowing that they are part of God's plan and purpose for my life helps me.

4. What does God use to remind us that nothing is too trivial or too great to escape His attention?
   Matthew 10:29—

John 19:10, 11—

It Is Often Hard to See God Working through Wicked People or Circumstances

5. Habakkuk 1:5–13 tells how wicked people in Judah's day would accomplish God's purpose. Explain how God's purposes can be accomplished through wicked people or circumstances.

6. When it appears that God does not intervene for us when He could have, we must remember He is working behind the scenes. What do Psalms 121:3 and 4 and 37:23 remind us about God?

7. Does God always arrange circumstances in our lives for our good? Read Romans 8:28 and 29. Explain your answer.

From MY Perspective—J. O.

"In every thing give thanks: for this is the will of God in Christ Jesus concerning you" (1 Thessalonians 5:18). Thank God for *everything?* When we first read that verse, it would seem God is asking us to do the impossible. And thanking God in everything would be impossible if we did not believe that God is working in every circumstance for our ultimate good. Often our main concern is to acquire more comfort; God's main concern is to build more character.

When we offer "the sacrifice of praise" (Hebrews 13:15) in

the midst of a trying circumstance, we can remember what God wants to teach us:

In tribulation—He teaches us patience (James 1:2–4).

When the heat is on—He teaches us that we can come forth as gold (Job 23:10).

When we are weak—He teaches us that we are the strongest spiritually when our own strength is weak (2 Corinthians 12:9).

When we are chastened—He teaches us how much He loves us (Hebrews 12:6).

When we wait—He teaches us how to renew our strength (Isaiah 40:31).

Which do you want more, *comfort* or *character?*

God Does What He Pleases, When He Pleases, and How He Pleases

8. How could Psalm 115:1–3 and Isaiah 46:10 help you answer the confused and questioning person who asks, "Where was God when that happened?"

9. Job came to grips with God's sovereignty in Job 42:2. What does this verse mean to you?

10. Read Isaiah 14:27 and Daniel 4:35. Does the fact that God does as He pleases make you fearful, or does it cause you to trust Him even more? Why?

11. Reread Romans 8:28 and 29 and read 1 Thessalonians 4:1. What is God's ultimate purpose for all believers?

12. Read Ephesians 2:10. What else was part of God's plan for every believer when He created us?

13. See Jeremiah 29:11. God has another plan for us; what is it?

From MY Perspective—Juanita

Jeremiah 29:11 is such an encouragement to me when I think of the sovereignty of God: "For I know the thoughts that I think toward you, saith the LORD, thoughts of peace, and not of evil, to give you an expected end." God's plans are to prosper me and not to harm me and to give me hope and a future. I like to think of that as a hopeful future. Although I know these words were written to the people of Judah in their captivity, I know they are for me as well. God says, "For whatsoever things were written aforetime were written for our learning, that we through patience and comfort of the scriptures might have hope" (Romans 15:4).

I like these thoughts from the *Streams in the Desert* devotional:

> *In the center of the circle*
> *Of the Will of God I stand:*
> *There can come no second causes,*
> *All must come from His dear hand.*
> *All is well! for 'tis my Father*
> *Who my life hath planned.*[2]

Does God Permit Evil?

14. If you read Genesis 37—50, you will see an unusual story unfold. It is the story of Joseph's being sold into slavery by his evil brothers. Joseph was abused and mistreated, yet in time he could see that through his brothers' actions God was working on his behalf. What did he say to his brothers when he saw them years later? Read Genesis 45:8 and 50:20.

15. We know from the account of Joseph that God sometimes uses the sinful actions of men to accomplish His purposes.

Does this mean that God puts the evil thoughts into their minds? Read James 1:13 and 14. Explain your answer.

16. God allows us to make sinful choices, but He will hold us accountable for the choices we make. In what way will we pay the consequences? See Galatians 6:7 and Psalm 62:12.

17. Why is it so hard for us to fully comprehend the sovereignty of God? Read Psalm 50:21 and Isaiah 55:7 and 8.

From MY Perspective—J. O.

I do not have any easy answers on how to handle your trials when God doesn't make sense. There is no twelve-step program with quick answers for suffering saints! But I can recommend to you some precious promises that will change your attitude about suffering. This change of attitude will allow you to transcend your problems and "mount up with wings as eagles" (Isaiah 40:31).

I would encourage you to memorize the verses listed on pages 24 and 25. I call them "TNT" (Tried 'n' True) verses. These verses have been tried and found true in my life. If you have no adversity in your life, you may feel you do not need them. Let me remind you, it is much easier to accept and appreciate the sovereignty of God when life is good and God seems to make sense. When adversity charges into my life, my mind is often dull and full of confusing questions, making concentration hard.

I would also encourage you to be careful not to bang people over the head with Romans 8:28 when their world has just fallen apart. They are not in a state of mind to accept the value of this verse at that time in their lives.

Tried 'n' True Verses

Isaiah 26:3 and 4

"Thou wilt keep him in perfect peace, whose mind is stayed on thee: because he trusteth in thee. Trust ye in the LORD for ever: for in the LORD JEHOVAH is everlasting strength."

Psalm 34:18 and 19

"The LORD is nigh unto them that are of a broken heart; and saveth such as be of a contrite spirit. Many are the afflictions of the righteous: but the LORD delivereth him out of them all."

1 Corinthians 10:13

"There hath no temptation taken you but such as is common to man: but God is faithful, who will not suffer you to be tempted above that ye are able; but will with the temptation also make a way to escape, that ye may be able to bear it."

2 Corinthians 12:9

"And he said unto me, My grace is sufficient for thee: for my strength is made perfect in weakness. Most gladly therefore will I rather glory in my infirmities, that the power of Christ may rest upon me."

Hebrews 13:5 and 6

"Let your conversation be without covetousness; and be content with such things as ye have: for he hath said, I will never leave thee, nor forsake thee. So that we may boldly say, The Lord is my helper, and I will not fear what man shall do unto me."

Isaiah 40:31

"But they that wait upon the LORD shall renew their strength; they shall mount up with wings as eagles; they shall run, and not be weary; and they shall walk, and not faint."

Isaiah 41:10

"Fear thou not; for I am with thee: be not dismayed; for I am thy God: I will strengthen thee; yea, I will help thee; yea, I will uphold thee with the right hand of my righteousness."

From YOUR Perspective

Have you accepted the fact that God is sovereign? He does as He pleases, and He plans your life as He pleases. When you read Genesis 18:25, how do you react? "Shall not the Judge of all the earth do right?" Does one side of your brain say, "Yes," while the other side of your brain says, "But it isn't fair!" If you feel God has been unfair with you, will you pray this prayer?

> *Lord, I know You are sovereign. I know You can and will do as You please in my life. Forgive me for feeling You have been unfair in the things You have allowed in my life.*
>
> *Lord, I know You are concerned about my ultimate good—to become more like Jesus Christ. Thank You for being that intimately concerned about my life. I know You will do what is right, even if it does not look right to me. Thank You for not giving up on me.*

Notes:

1. Hannah Whitall Smith, *The Christian's Secret of a Happy Life* (Westwood, NJ, Fleming H. Revell, 1952), 146.

2. *Streams in the Desert* (Grand Rapids: Zondervan Publishing House, 1965), August 14.

Don't Doubt in the Dark What You Know in the Light!

GOD doesn't usually answer our question, "Why are You allowing this to happen?" However, He does give us some answers as to why He allows adversity into our lives. All adversity revolves around one central theme—growth.

God wants us to grow up, just as we want our children to grow. However, God's goal in our growth differs from the physical and mental growth we want for our children. God's main concern for us is spiritual maturity. As parents or teachers we learn and become better able to help our children grow physically, emotionally, mentally, and even spiritually; but God already knows perfectly how to help us grow spiritually. He knows that the fastest route to spiritual maturity is down the highway marked Testings and Adversities.

An individual could not possibly appreciate the value of trials in his or her life if that person did not understand God's purpose. God knew we would have questions when nothing seems to make sense in our lives. He also knew we would have a tendency to forget what we know when the heat is on. We all have probably heard the statement "Don't doubt in the dark what you know in the light." That's what this lesson is all about. We want to try to help you remember what you know about God when nothing else makes sense.

Let's look at several verses to remind us that He knows what He is doing. *We,* too, can know what He is doing—if we go with what we know instead of how we feel.

"He Knows" Verses

Job 23:10

"But He knoweth the way that I take: when he hath tried me, I shall come forth as gold."

1. What do we *know* God is wanting to do in our lives? Consider 2 Timothy 2:20 and 21.

Psalm 1:6

"For the LORD knoweth the way of the righteous: but the way of the ungodly shall perish."

2. The word "knoweth" in this verse means "an intimate relationship." God knows us so intimately that He even orders our steps and stops (Psalm 37:23). How does Psalm 1:6 help you when nothing else makes sense to you?

Matthew 6:8

"For your Father knoweth what things ye have need of, before ye ask him."

3. Do you need peace? Do you need contentment? Do you need a spirit of acceptance? Do you need to forgive? God knows all your needs. What has He promised to do for you in Philippians 4:19?

Deuteronomy 2:7

"For the LORD thy God hath blessed thee in all the works of thy hand: he knoweth thy walking through this great wilderness."

4. We know this verse was written to the Children of Israel during their wilderness wanderings. Since our God never changes, what do we know He will do for us?

From MY Perspective—Juanita

Our Heavenly Father cares when He sees us wandering in a wilderness of doubt and confusion. He cares when we are hanging on for dear life in the midst of a blinding storm. He allows these times because He knows our faith grows best when it is tried. He holds our hand in the wilderness and in the storm, but He begs us not to try to see the next step we are to take. He wants us, instead, to trust His wisdom and knowledge: "O the depth of the riches both of the wisdom and knowledge of God! how unsearchable are his judgments, and his ways past finding out!" (Romans 11:33).

He who guides a hundred million stars in the universe knows the way through the wilderness and the storm. He has promised, "I will never leave thee, nor forsake thee" (Hebrews 13:5).

Have you ever been in that wilderness of doubt and confusion? I have! Did God ever forsake you; did He ever fail you? I'm sure your answer is the same as mine. No, He never left me; He never failed me. Sometimes when it was dark, it seemed as though He had left me or failed me; but when the sun began to shine again, I knew that wasn't true. I knew that He was stretching my faith again and pushing me into another level of spiritual maturity. I often have to remind myself during these times, "Don't doubt in the dark what you know in the light." I would encourage you to do the same.

Jeremiah 29:11

"For I know the thoughts that I think toward you, saith the LORD, thoughts of peace, and not of evil, to give you an expected end."

5. God is concerned about today and tomorrow in our lives. Another version of Jeremiah 29:11 translates "an expected end" as "a future and a hope." What do we *know* He has planned for us?

God has given us some great "He knows" verses. He has also given us several "we know" verses.

"We Know" Verses

James 1:2–4

"My brethren, count it all joy when ye fall into divers temptations; knowing this, that the trying of your faith worketh patience. But let patience have her perfect work, that ye may be perfect and entire, wanting nothing."

6. What three things do we know God wants us to experience as a result of our trials?

Romans 5:3 and 4

"And not only so, but we glory in tribulations also: knowing that tribulation worketh patience; and patience, experience; and experience, hope."

7. These verses seem to indicate that tribulation, or trials, is a process with a purpose. What do we know about the process and the purpose?

From MY Perspective—J. O.

We often read the little saying, "Be patient; God isn't finished with me yet!" and smile. However, that thought holds a lot of truth. God planned for the Christian life to be one of continuous growth. In a sense we are all still "under construction." God grows a mushroom overnight, but it takes a long time to grow a strong oak.

We all want to be like a strong oak instead of a mushroom, but we rarely appreciate the process needed for growth. In fact, we often resist it. We know that adversities will help us grow spiritually, but we tend to focus on the circumstances surrounding the adversity, rather than looking by faith to what God is trying to accomplish in our lives. We must look beyond the adversity and know "that tribulation worketh patience; and patience, experience; and experience, hope." The trials will teach us to endure patiently the hardships of life and not run from them. This patient endurance will develop a godly character in us that learns "to hope against hope." We must just keep hoping when all outward signs of hope have vanished.

> *I do not know, I cannot see,*
> *What God's kind hand prepares for me,*
> *Nor can my glance pierce through the haze*
> *Which covers all my future ways;*
> *But yet I know that o'er it all*
> *Rules He who notes the sparrow's fall.*[1]

Psalm 119:75

"I know, O LORD, that thy judgments are right, and that thou in faithfulness hast afflicted me."

8. Sometimes the things God allows in our lives seem unfair. What do we know about God that can assure us that this seeming unfairness is not true? See Genesis 18:25.

2 Corinthians 5:1

"For we know that if our earthly house of this tabernacle were dissolved, we have a building of God, an house not made with hands, eternal in the heavens."

9. What do we know about our journey here on earth that can give us hope for the future?

Jeremiah 10:23

"O LORD, I know that the way of man is not in himself: it is not in man that walketh to direct his steps."

10. When I think I know how to run my life better than God, what do I need to remember?

Romans 8:28

"And we know that all things work together for good to them that love God, to them who are the called according to his purpose."

11. Read Romans 8:28 and 29. What do we know is the ultimate good God wants to accomplish in our lives?

From MY Perspective—Juanita

Don't doubt in the dark what you know in the light! Go with what you know is true about God. Think about the promises of God instead of your problems. Take a minute right now to meditate on three things you know about God. What three words came to your mind? When I start thinking about my God, I know He is trustworthy, patient, faithful, loving, all-powerful, good, forgiving, tenderhearted—and the list goes on and on.

When a hound dog is tracking something and loses its scent, the dog hunts backward until it finds the scent again. When it finds the scent, it pursues its game with an even louder bark than before. When life seems confusing and you're losing your sense of direction, back up and go with what you know about God. Rehearse the attributes of God. Humans may change, but we know our God will never change. He is our rock, our fortress, our deliverer, our strength, our high tower (Psalm 18:2). Don't doubt in the dark what you know in the light!

12. In the midst of an adversity, have you ever forgotten what you know about God? What was the result of your negative response?

13. What have you learned in this lesson that can help you know how to respond to your adversities in a way that is pleasing to God?

14. What does God know about you that you are glad no one else knows?

15. What do you know about God that you can cling to when nothing else makes sense?

16. What has God allowed in your life this past year to help you grow spiritually? How did you respond to it? Have you seen any spiritual growth as a result? Explain your answer.

From MY Perspective—J. O.

Yes, adversities are from God and for our good. We all know that when life is smooth and easy, we rarely make any giant steps of faith. Adversity has a way of bringing us to our knees and forcing us to get into the Word of God. I know that adversity has forced me to take some steps of faith that have resulted in my biggest gains spiritually. We must remember our adversity alone is not good, but it "work[s] together for good." Our adversities, mixed with other circumstances, can end up being good if they draw us closer to Christ and if others begin to see something different about our lives.

> *We climbed the path by the zigzag path*
> *And wondered why—until*
> *We understood it was made zigzag*
> *To break the force of the hill.*
>
> *A road straight up would prove too steep*
> *For the traveler's feet to tread;*
> *The thought was kind in its wise design*
> *Of a zigzag path instead.*
>
> *It is often so in our daily life;*
> *We fail to understand*
> *That the twisting way our feet tread*
> *By love alone was planned.*
>
> *Then murmur not at the winding way,*
> *It is our Father's will*
> *To lead us Home by the zigzag path,*
> *To break the force of the hill.*[2]

Begin to imagine how God can transform your zigzag path into something of value and purpose in your life. Someday you will look back and know that path was the best way. He wants us to advance through our adversities, not run from them!

From YOUR Perspective

Have you forgotten in the dark what you knew in the light? When nothing seemed to make sense, did you forget all the things you knew about the goodness of God and His promises to provide for you? If you have been stumbling in darkness, will you pray this prayer?

> *Lord, forgive me for becoming so consumed with my problems that I almost forgot all Your precious promises to me and for me. Renew and revive my dull mind. Help me to dwell on Your promises instead of my problems. I know You have allowed these adversities to draw me closer to You and to conform me to the image of Your Son.*
>
> *Lord, I want godly character more than an easy, comfortable life. Help me not to doubt in the dark what I know in the light!*

Notes:
1. Author unknown.
2. Author unknown.

Part 2

Questions We Ask
When Life Doesn't Make Sense

How Can I Handle All This Stress?

I DON'T think our grandparents ever used words such as "stressed out" or "burnout." These are modern-day terms developed for the "aspirin age" we live in. One person calls stress "hurry sickness"; another person calls it the "hurry-worry syndrome." Stress has become a way of life in many homes: instant dinners, the telephone constantly ringing, the endless noise of the TV, blaring music, continual arguments and shouting matches, too many bills, and not enough sleep. Add to this already stressful mess all the stress people have at the workplace, and you have men and women who are existing on aspirin and tranquilizers to make it through the day.

We all are a part of this stress-filled world, a world full of confusion, uncertainty, change, misunderstanding. The key to learning to live in a stress-filled world without being stressed is to learn to manage our stress.

This lesson is for people who are stretched to the limit and often feel exhausted and worn out, even when they love what they are doing. If this doesn't describe you, I'm sure you know someone who fits this description. Why not pass this lesson on to him or her? In this lesson we want to look at the harmful results of too much stress and what we can do to relieve some of it.

What Is Stress Anyway?

Not all stress is harmful. Stress can be a great motivator. It can also relieve boredom and loneliness. However, stress overload can be harmful, especially if one experiences it for long periods of time.

1. Perhaps no other person in the Bible had more stress than David. Read Psalm 18:29. How was his stress positive and helpful?

2 Read Psalm 42:3–6. How was David's stress negative and harmful?

From MY Perspective—Juanita

Psychologists class people as Type A and Type B personalities. Type A's are high achievers. They always want to achieve more in less time. Therefore, they are more prone toward stress overload. We could call Type A's racehorses and Type B's turtles. Type B's rarely experience stress; they are laid back, are never in a hurry, and seldom worry.

My husband and I are both Type A personalities. Sometimes this combination is good, and many times it is bad. Added to my personality, I have to take medication for an overactive thyroid. These two conditions have caused much stress in my life. In fact, a few years ago I was on the verge of burnout. I know the harmful and helpful effects of stress.

As I write this, I am just recovering from another bout of stress overload. I am really disappointed with myself that I am such a slow learner in this area of my life. I think I am finally learning how much stress I can handle before it begins to affect me physically. I am learning the hard way, as most of us do, that stress will always be there, but God is always there as well. With God's help and strength I am learning to slow down more and to rush and fuss less. First Peter 5:7 really works: "Casting *all your care* upon him; for he careth for you" (emphasis added).

3. Read Luke 10:38–42. Who could have been a Type A personality and who a Type B personality? What makes you think so?

4. No doubt Martha was stressed out by the time Christ arrived, and she could not enjoy His presence. What did she say to Christ in verse 40?

5. What undue stresses do we often put on ourselves when we have guests in our homes?

6. Most of our stress is caused by how we react to problems, not the problem itself. Mary was not Martha's problem. What was causing Martha's stress? See verse 41.

7. In verse 42 Jesus seemed to be telling Martha not to let the good take the place of the best. What do Type A people often neglect? Consider Psalm 46:10.

From MY Perspective—J. O.

Are you a Type A person? If so, then you are a prime candidate for stress overload. You need to be aware of its symptoms. A stretched rubber band can help illustrate too much stress. When you take a rubber band and stretch it out between your fingers, it stays tight until you release it so that it can return to its normal unstretched position. The same happens in the human body's stress responses when a body is stretched by demands or emergencies. However, if you take that same rubber band and keep it stretched for a prolonged period, it will not return to the normal relaxed position; it will stay stretched or will break. Continual stress overload does the same thing to our bodies and minds, and we end up with physical and psychological consequences.

When someone stays in prolonged periods of stress, his or her body responds like the stretched-out rubber band and remains in a continual "fight or flight" stage. The person's system is bathed in adrenaline, which causes this state of arousal in his system and disrupts the normal body functions. This is why his blood pressure stays up and the muscle tension continues even when the stress seems to be gone.

In my thirty-two years as a pastor, I often experienced times of prolonged stress. I learned early in my ministry that if I did not handle my stresses, they would handle me. Stress starts in our minds and ends up in our bodies. The key to relieving stress is keeping your mind stress free. Philippians 2:5–8 has been a great help to me, especially verse 5: "Let this mind be in you, which was also in Christ Jesus."

Symptoms of Stress Overload and How It Affects the Human Body

Brain

8. How does too much stress affect the brain? See Proverbs 4:16; Daniel 6:14, 18–20; and Hebrews 12:3.

Heart

9. Read James 3:14. What do stressful situations create in your heart? Why are these feelings harmful to you physically?

Stomach

10. Elijah had a lot of stress in his life; Jezebel had threatened to

kill him. How did the stress affect his stomach? Read 1 Kings 19:4–8.

11. Stress causes people to overeat or not want to eat at all. What stomach problems occur as a result of too much stress?

Muscles

12. Before David finally confessed his sin with Bathsheba, his life was filled with stress and tension. What did all the tension do to the muscles in his body? Read Psalm 32:3 and 4 to discover the answer.

13. What areas of the human body generally feel the results of muscle tension first?

Lungs

14. How do you think stress overload would affect the lungs?

Identify the Source of Stress in Your Life

15. Read Exodus 18:18. What was Moses' problem?

16. Is overwork causing stress in your life? In what way?

17. According to 1 Samuel 30:6, what was David's problem?

18. Are your enemies causing stress in your life? In what way?

19. What other problems did David have? See 2 Samuel 11:2–5.

20. Is immorality or the temptation to immorality causing stress in your life? In what way?

21. Read Jonah 1:2, 3, and 7 and 2:1 and 2. What caused the stress and affliction in Jonah's life?

22. Is running from the Lord causing stress in your life? In what way?

From MY Perspective—Juanita

What is the end result of living in a continual state of stress overload? Burnout! People often ignore it in its early stages, because burned out people are usually self-sufficient, competent people who hide their weaknesses rather well. However, eventually the state of fatigue and frustration leaves them running on empty. What happens is similar to what takes place when a car is running on two cylinders instead of eight. The end result is a person depleted of physical and mental resources. The main thing a burned out person needs is enough rest time for physical and mental resources to be revived.

A few years ago I got myself so busy grazing in God's green pastures that I forgot to slow down and rest once in a while. I was so busy with my commitments to my husband, my family, my church, and my writing that I was out of touch with my feelings and my needs. I was running on empty and needed to rest, so the Lord stopped me in my tracks. After the doctor told me I was on the verge of burnout, I had to change my lifestyle and do nothing but rest for a while. During that time Psalm 23:2 became very real to me: "He maketh me to lie down in green pastures." If we are not smart enough to slow down on our own, God will slow us down for us.

Steps to Reduce Stress Overload

STEP ONE: Learn to Trust God

23. Ask yourself the following questions:

    • Am I trying to live beyond my limitations—financially, mentally, emotionally, and physically? Am I content with what God has given me? (Consider Philippians 4:11.)

    • Am I constantly living under deadlines? Reevaluate your schedule to relieve time pressures and try to simplify your life a bit.

    • Am I carrying extra baggage in the form of anger, resentment, anxiety, or bitterness? Unload this junk now! (Read Matthew 6:14 and 15.)

    • Am I a driven person? Do I do what I do because people expect it, because I enjoy it and it fulfills me, or because I try to impress others? (Read Psalm 37:4 and 5.)

STEP TWO: Evaluate Your Lifestyle
Exercise

24. According to 1 Corinthians 6:19 and 20, why is it important to take care of our bodies?

25. Timothy tells us that exercise profits a little (1 Timothy 4:8). Exercise is not the greatest reducer of stress, but it is one of the important stress reducers. Why do you think exercise would reduce stress?

Nutrition

26. How do busy, stressful schedules affect our eating habits? How does Romans 12:2 apply to our eating habits?

Rest and Relaxation

27. When we are too busy and stressed out, what are the first things we stop doing? See Mark 6:31.

28. What do you do for relaxation? When do you do it? Do you have a daily time to rest and relax? When?

29. We must learn to trust God and slow down long enough to see what we are doing with our lives. In Jeremiah 17:5–8 we see a contrast between a cursed person and a blessed person. Who is cursed, and what is the result of his lifestyle?

30. Who is blessed, or happy, and what is the result of his lifestyle?

From MY Perspective—J. O.

I think we would all agree that good nutrition and regular exercise balanced with work and rest should be our goal. To accomplish this goal, we need to be careful that we do not let ourselves get involved in back-to-back high-stress projects. Our minds and bodies need time to recuperate. Our lives should look like a picture of hills and valleys. Every mountainous, stressful situation should be followed by a valley time to mend. Every day should end with a calming of the mind and body. Each week should have a rest time.

I have learned that rest is more than sleep and lying around doing nothing. True rest comes from a restful, contented spirit. Paul wrote, "I have learned, in whatsoever state I am, therewith to be content" (Philippians 4:11). When we learn to trust God, we find ourselves content with His appointments in our lives. We are not always striving for something more, but are happy with what He provides (v. 19).

The greatest rest comes to our soul when we obey. Psalm 46:10 confirms this idea: "Be still, and know that I am God." These Hebrew words signify more than quietness and meditating in God's presence; they mean letting tension go out of your life. Begin meditating on some of the attributes of God: He is almighty; He is a comforter; He is faithful; He is long-suffering; He is powerful. Will you slow down, relax, and trust God?

Let me emphasize again that rest is more than sleep; we need a restful, contented spirit.

From YOUR Perspective

Do you feel that your life is out of control? Have you been running on empty? Are you ready to slow down long enough to listen to God and do what your body is telling you? If so, would you pray this prayer?

> *Lord, I need to make some changes in my life now. I need Your help! Give me wisdom to slow down where I can and to change where I must. Give me courage to say yes when I should say yes and no when I should say, "No, I can't take on anything else right now."*
>
> *Lord, help me to set aside all my busyness, thoughts, and jobs to be done long enough to spend time in Your presence and hear You whisper, "Be still, and know that I am God."*

How Can I Keep from Worrying?

ONE leading physician stated that 70 percent of all patients who go to doctors could cure themselves if they would only quit their fears and worries. The Greek meaning for the word "worry" is "to divide the mind." Worry divides the mind between damaging thoughts and good thoughts. James 1:8 states, "A double minded man is unstable in *all his ways*" (emphasis added). He is unstable in his thought processes, emotions, judgments, and decisions. The worrier robs himself of peace by dividing his mind.

For years we have encouraged people to read the Twenty-third Psalm as a prescription for peace in the midst of turmoil. This psalm was written to God's people, "the sheep of his pasture" (Psalm 100:3). It was written by a shepherd, David, who understood the nature of sheep. He viewed himself as a weak, defenseless, foolish sheep. He saw God, the Shepherd, as his provider, protector, and deliverer. His Shepherd was everything he would ever need. Notice the intimacy he had with the Shepherd and the solid certainty he enjoyed in this relationship: "The LORD is *my* shepherd; *I* shall not want" (Psalm 23:1; emphasis added). He was under the care of Jehovah, and so are you, if you are one of "the sheep of his pasture."

Do you need a closer relationship with the Shepherd and a solid certainty that He will be everything you will ever need? If so, here is our prescription for "Winning over Worry in a Week":

Read the Twenty-third Psalm five times a day for seven days. Don't just quote it from memory, but slowly read it and think through each verse. Then sometime during each day, study a portion of this lesson.

Rx for Worry
Read the psalm before breakfast.
Read it after breakfast.
Read it at lunchtime.
Read it at dinnertime.
Read it at bedtime.

Winning over Worry in a Week

DAY ONE: The Lord Has Plans for You
"The LORD is my shepherd; I shall not want" (Psalm 23:1).

1. How does a shepherd plan ahead for his sheep?

2. What has your Shepherd planned for your life? Read John 10:10, 14, 15, and 27–29 and Psalm 55:22.

3. Read Jeremiah 29:11. God has wonderful plans for His children. How could this verse help free you from worry?

4. What do the words "I shall not want" picture?

From MY Perspective—J. O.

I once heard someone say, "Sheep never carry burdens; others do, but not sheep." Christ says that we are the sheep of His pasture (Psalm 100:3) and that He is our shepherd (Psalm 23:1).

"The LORD is my shepherd; I shall not want." What a wonderful promise! Do you believe it? Do you act as if you believe it? Are you wanting, whining, and worrying? Or trusting, thankful, and tranquil? Who is our Shepherd? He is the almighty creator, the Lord God of Heaven and earth, the One Who holds the universe in His hand as though it were a tiny object. He is our shepherd and has declared Himself to be our caretaker and keeper. If our minds could fully comprehend the greatness of our God and if our hearts could believe it, we would never have a fear or worry again. With such a Shepherd, how could we ever lack any good thing?

Remember, sheep never carry burdens—that's the shepherd's job. Are you carrying your burdens? Have you forgotten you have a Shepherd Who wants to do that for you? This poem is a good reminder for us:

> *It is God's will that I should cast*
> *On Him my care each day;*
> *He also bids me not to cast*
> *My confidence away.*
> *But, oh! I am so stupid, that*
> *When taken unawares,*
> *I cast away my confidence,*
> *And carry all my cares.*[1]

DAY TWO: The Lord Will Provide for You

"He maketh me to lie down in green pastures: he leadeth me beside the still waters" (Psalm 23:2).

5. Only contented sheep lie down in green pastures. Read Psalm 95:7–11. Why is it that some of God's children never enjoy the contented, restful life in green pastures?

6. Read Psalm 100. How could these verses relate to Psalm 23:2 and free you from worry?

DAY THREE: The Lord Can Keep You Going

"He restoreth my soul" (Psalm 23:3a).

7. Worry weighs us down and wears us out physically. When we lose our joy, it is hard to keep going. In Psalm 51 David was burdened with his sin. Have you ever seen your worry as sin?

8. What does God want to restore in your soul when you sin? How will it be restored? See Psalm 51:12 and then verses 1 to 3.

9. When you confess your worry as sin, God will restore your joy. How can you keep this joy flowing from your life each day? See John 15:4, 5, and 11 and Isaiah 26:3.

DAY FOUR: The Lord Will Lead You Right

"He leadeth me in the paths of righteousness for his name's sake" (Psalm 23:3b).

10. Is a Christian walking right when his or her life is filled with worry? Explain your answer.

11. How does worry affect God's reputation in the eyes of those who are watching a believer who worries?

12. Read Isaiah 30:21 and Proverbs 3:5 and 6. How does God want us to walk?

13. What happens when we will not let God lead us? Read Isaiah 48:18.

DAY FIVE: The Lord Will Take Care of You

"Yea, though I walk through the valley of the shadow of death, I will fear no evil: for thou art with me; thy rod and thy staff they comfort me" (Psalm 23:4).

14. Do you worry about dangerous or difficult experiences that you fear you may have to endure? What is the remedy for your fears and worries? Read Habakkuk 3:16–19.

15. How can you change your thoughts from worry to trust? Read Psalm 119:11, 18, 71, 97, 164, and 176.

From MY Perspective—Juanita

During his valley experiences of life, David encouraged himself in his Shepherd's care for him: "For thou art with me." He was not afraid of the future. He did not imagine fearful things happening, for he wrote, "I will fear no evil."

I once read an interesting statement that characterizes us so accurately: "If we didn't have any troubles except the ones that really happen, we would only have a tenth of our present burdens. We feel a thousand deaths in fearing one." How does this observation relate to you?

Those of us who have been through dark valley experiences realize that during them we discovered a new source of strength and courage that can be found only in God. As we look back and see how our faith was multiplied in the valley, we have no fear of the future. We know that we will not walk down that dark road alone: "I will fear no evil: for thou art with me."

How do you cope with the adversities that come your way? With Christ, the Good Shepherd, you can face them calmly. With Him guiding your life, you can face them fearlessly. I'm striving for that daily. What about you?

> *I do not know what next may come*
> *Across my pilgrim way;*
> *I do not know tomorrow's road,*
> *Nor see beyond today.*
> *But this I know—My Savior knows*
> *The path I cannot see;*
> *And I can trust His wounded hand*
> *To guide and care for me.*[2]

DAY SIX: The Lord Will Bless You

"Thou preparest a table before me in the presence of mine enemies: thou anointest my head with oil; my cup runneth over" (Psalm 23:5).

16. The Lord wants to bless us with a spirit of confidence in the midst of those who criticize, condemn, and correct us. Why do we experience worry and fear instead of calmness and confidence? Consider Isaiah 30:15b and 21.

17. "Anointing" in the Hebrew-Christian tradition means "the healing of the Lord; the blessing and joy of the Lord." "Cup" in the Hebrew means "my life." Describe the person whose cup is running over. Then read Psalm 5:11 and 12.

From MY Perspective—J. O.

The youngest daughter in a pastor's home was being disciplined for a minor offense; she was required to eat her dinner alone at her little table in a corner of the dining room. The rest of the family ignored her, until they heard her praying, "I thank Thee, Lord, for preparing a table before me in the presence of mine enemies."

Sometimes life seems tough for children. As we become adults, we learn that life is tough! We can expect some bruises, and that's just the way it will be. Our hearts will be broken; feelings will get hurt; we'll be dealt some harsh, sharp blows. The tender Shepherd understands our hurts and is always ready to minister to those hurts and to put a song back into our hearts. The psalmist wrote, "Thou anointest my head with oil; my cup runneth over."

How can our cup just keep running over with joy when there is so much hurt and pain all around us or in our own lives? God is the eternal wellspring of our joy. Our hearts are at ease, and we live a wonderful life full of joy when we draw upon His strength each day. Our Shepherd puts a song into our hearts and a spring in our step. We no longer have to live in worry and fear, because He surrounds us. We are under the shelter of Heaven!

"For thou, LORD, wilt bless the righteous; with favour wilt thou compass him as with a shield" (Psalm 5:12).

DAY SEVEN: The Lord Follows You

"Surely goodness and mercy shall follow me all the days of my life: and I will dwell in the house of the LORD for ever" (Psalm 23:6).

18. The Shepherd continually follows His sheep, wanting to give them goodness and mercy. Describe some of the aspects of God's goodness to us.

    Ephesians 4:32—

    Philippians 4:13–19—

    Isaiah 26:3—

19. Read Psalm 78:42; Genesis 18:25; and Hebrews 12:5–8. Describe God's mercy.

20. How does God's mercy affect you?

21. Do you ever worry about your eternal relationship with God and worry that you might lose your salvation? How can you be sure that you have eternal life and will never lose it? Read Romans 10:9, 10, and 13 for the answer.

From MY Perspective—Juanita

Did you know that Christians have guardian angels? "The angel of the LORD encampeth round about them that fear him, and delivereth them," states Psalm 34:7. Could it be that our guardian angels are called "goodness" and "mercy"? They follow us and surround us every day of our lives. They are there on the festive days as well as on the frustrating days; on our bright days and dark days; on our delightful days and dreary days.

"Goodness" supplies every need we shall ever have so that we can always say, "I shall not want [lack]."

"Mercy" corrects us when we go astray so that we can say, "Thy rod and thy staff they comfort me."

The Lord Is My Shepherd

Yes, the Lord is my shepherd; I never have to worry or want because . . .

• The Lord has plans for me. I will have everything I need under His good care and management.

• The Lord will provide for me. I can be content. I never have to feel empty; my thirst will be quenched.

• The Lord will keep me going. He restores me and lifts me up when I feel I cannot keep going.

• The Lord will lead me right. I never have to fear the path ahead when He guides me.

• The Lord will take care of me. No matter what dark valley I pass through, I will never be alone.

• The Lord wants to bless me. The Lord has a full and overflowing life planned for me.

• The Lord will follow me. Goodness and mercy will be my constant companions on earth, and Heaven is assured for my future.

From YOUR Perspective

It is a great relief to put the tangles of life into God's hands and leave them there. Are you doing that? Will you? If so, will you pray this prayer?

Lord, forgive me for whining, wanting, and worrying. I desire to learn to trust You with every area of my life. When I begin to fill up with anxiety and fear, help me to remember to read the Twenty-third Psalm five times a day until I begin to experience Your peace and rest in my soul.

Notes:

1. *Springs in the Valley* (Grand Rapids: Zondervan Publishing House, 1968), December 5.

2. Margaret Clarkson, *Climbing the Heights* (Grand Rapids: Zondervan Publishing House, 1956), July 29.

I'm Battling Bitterness— Isn't That Normal?

HAVE you been hurt by some nasty experience in life? Have you let yourself become bitter? What is bitterness? It could easily be defined with two words—"harbored hurt." Every time we see the word "bitterness" in the New Testament, it comes from the same Greek root *pic,* which means "to cut, to prick." Bitterness is an angry feeling that pierces the heart, robbing a person of peace and blinding him or her to God's blessings.

Sometimes we can't avoid being hurt by someone. But we do not have to become bitter toward that person. If you find yourself wanting to avoid someone else, you may have a "harbored hurt" that you have not dealt with.

In this lesson we want to look at some of the causes for bitterness and consider ways to help free ourselves from this ugly sin.

1. How do we know that having a bitter spirit is sin? Read Hebrews 12:15.

2. Does a person have to tell you that he or she has a bitter spirit? Explain your answer. Also see Luke 6:45.

Causes for Bitterness

Sexual Abuse

3. Read 2 Samuel 13:1–22. What happened to Tamar?

4. Tamar was humiliated and broken. Read 2 Samuel 13:20. How did her brother Absalom add to her hurt?

5. Tamar most likely ended up a bitter lady. What did Absalom do to encourage her in her bitterness? Read 2 Samuel 13:22, 28, and 29.

6. Read Jeremiah 31:3. People who are sexually abused often feel that they no longer deserve anyone's love and that even God could no longer love them. Describe God's love for us.

From MY Perspective—Juanita

Absalom told Tamar, "Don't take this thing to heart." In other words, he told her just to be quiet. Obviously he did not understand the depth of emotional pain she was experiencing. She knew the disgrace she would face because of the social stigma associated with sexual abuse. Ammon, the one who committed the sin, should have been disgraced and treated as an outcast; but it was Tamar, the one sinned against, who ended up living in her brother's home, a desolate woman.

Even in our day of sexual promiscuity and liberty, many victims of sexual abuse end up retreating from others because of their feelings of unworthiness and shame.

I have never experienced sexual abuse, but I have counseled with many who have; and often they say they felt dirty, ugly, and valueless. They felt angry and bitter because they thought they were no longer worthy of love. However, that awful pattern of thinking was changed, little by little, after they understood that God loves them and that Christ died for all their ugly sins (Romans 5:8). How liberating it is for them to know that when God forgives, He never sees their sin again (1 John 1:9; Psalm 103:12). Accepting God's love and forgiveness set them free from their bitterness and also allowed them to express forgiveness to their offenders. Is there someone you need to forgive so that you can be set free?

Life's Injustices

7. When a person feels unfairly treated, at whom does the so-called offended one often aim his or her feelings? Read Job 27:2.

8. How can we overcome bitterness that stems from feelings of being treated unfairly? See Psalm 18:30 and Deuteronomy 32:4.

Difficult Circumstances

9. List some difficult circumstances people have had to endure.

10. Job 21:25 refers to a person who died in bitterness of soul, never having enjoyed anything good. How could this situation happen to a person living in a difficult circumstance?

11. How do Psalms 68:19 and 40:8 relate to the problem of bitterness?

From MY Perspective—J. O.

Humanly speaking, Fanny Crosby had every right to be bitter. At the age of six weeks she was blinded as a result of a doctor's blunder. She could have felt that God was unfair in allowing such a thing to happen to her. She could have dwelled on her difficult circumstances, but she did not. At the age of eight she wrote,

> *O what a happy soul am I*
> *Although I cannot see,*
> *I am resolved that in this world*
> *Contented I will be.*
> *How many blessings I enjoy*
> *That other people don't!*
> *So weep and sigh because I'm blind,*
> *I cannot, and I won't!*

Fanny Crosby went on to write a multitude of hymns we still sing today. When you read the words of her songs, you notice that she always focused upon God and His wonderful works. Here's an example:

> *All the way my Savior leads me—*
> *What have I to ask beside?*
> *Can I doubt His tender mercy,*
> *Who thru life has been my Guide?*
> *Heav'nly peace, divinest comfort,*
> *Here by faith in Him to dwell!*
> *For I know, whate'er befall me,*
> *Jesus doeth all things well.*

How did she keep such a positive spirit in such a difficult circumstance? She kept her focus off herself and her circumstances and on the Lord. If we want to keep from having a "poor-me" bitter spirit, we must do the same thing.

Family Relationships

12. Read Hebrews 12:15. Why is bitterness so destructive?

13. What is usually at the root of a bitter spirit? Read Matthew 18:21–35.

14. Whom could the merciful king and the unmerciful servant be contrasted to in Ephesians 4:32?

15. Is there someone in your family against whom you have been harboring feelings of bitterness? Who is it? What are you going to do about it?

16. The unmerciful servant in Matthew 18 was delivered to the tormentors (v. 34) because he would not forgive after he had been forgiven so much. What kind of torment would a person experience who is unwilling to forgive?

From MY Perspective—Juanita

When we refuse to forgive, we will be "delivered . . . to the tormentors." When we live in the gall of bitterness, we build our own torture chamber in a mental concentration camp. It will destroy us emotionally and mentally.

Bitterness is also like a cancer. It destroys the soul just as much as cancer destroys the body. The only good thing about cancer is that it is not communicable, that it cannot harm others. However, bitterness is worse than cancer because its soul-rotting poison can infect others as well.

No doubt, someone studying this lesson lived in a home with extremely difficult circumstances. You have memories you wish you could forget. You may be harboring feelings of bitterness and anger toward one or both of your parents. If your parents were not abusive and ungodly in the way they handled situations, you have much for which to be thankful. Many parents are good but not always the most wise in how they deal with daily situations and problems. I like the way Rabbi Kushner expressed his thoughts on this subject.

> *We need to stop blaming our parents for having made mistakes in raising us. They were amateurs when it came to raising children—a task where even experts do not always know the answers. In their loving, faltering way, they gave us something more valuable than a perfect childhood. They taught us what a complicated thing love is, what a challenge it is to love and raise a child. And as we grow up and become parents ourselves, we grow to appreciate that.*[1]

Maybe you need to say to yourself, "Whatever happened in the past I cannot change. I will accept it as part of my past—it does not have to affect my future. It's okay for my parents to be who they are. I want to be the best I can be for my children."

How Can We Turn Bitterness Loose?

17. Bitterness is something we choose to keep in our lives. When we get hurt, we must deal with our feelings quickly before they get a chance to grow, "lest any root of bitterness [spring] up" (Hebrews 12:15). Bitterness grows quickly if it is not nipped in the bud. If it is not dealt with Biblically, it will result in more sin. Listed below are eight ways to deal with bitterness in a Biblical manner. Read the verses below and fill in the blanks.

(a) _____ is sin that will _____ not only us but others as well (Hebrews 12:15).

(b) We must confess our bitterness as sin if we want God's forgiveness and _____ (1 John 1:9).

(c) Instead of being bitter toward others, we must be _____, tenderhearted, and _____ (Ephesians 4:32).

(d) We must forgive others because _____ has forgiven us (Ephesians 4:32).

(e) We must forgive if we want God to _____ us (Matthew 6:14, 15).

(f) We must forgive if we want our prayers_____ (Psalm 66:18).

(g) We must see the circumstances that caused our bitterness as an opportunity for _____ growth (James 1:2–4).

(h) We must remember _____ is sovereign. He does as He _____ to teach us about His _____ in our lives (Psalm 135:6).

From MY Perspective—J. O.

As I have talked with people about their bitterness, they often say, "You just don't understand; you've never had to endure what I have. You don't know what they did to me." I must admit that is true, but I am so thankful I can point them to the One Who does understand, Jesus Christ our Savior. To identify with our emotional turmoil and deep feelings of hurt and pain, He left the splendor of Heaven and came to earth to be our healer. For us to identify with the emotional turmoil and pain He experienced for us, we need to walk through the Garden and to the cross with Him.

In the Garden the Savior cried, "My soul is exceeding sorrowful, even unto death" (Matthew 26:37, 38). He knows how you feel when you no longer want to live. Psalm 69:20 records Him saying, "Reproach hath broken my heart; and I am full of heaviness." Matthew 26:56 informs us that "all the disciples forsook him, and fled." The abuse and suffering He endured at His trial and crucifixion are beyond anything we can relate to. So when you say, "No one understands how badly I've been hurt," that just isn't true. Christ understands, and He cares! He is touched with the feeling of your hurt and pain, and He invites you to bring all your bitterness and resentment to Him. He wants to free you from these burdens. He willingly extends mercy and grace to help you in your time of need: "For we have not an high priest which cannot be touched with the feeling of our infirmities; but was in all points tempted like as we are, yet without sin. Let us therefore come boldly unto the throne of grace, that we may obtain mercy, and find grace to help in time of need" (Hebrews 4:15, 16).

From YOUR Perspective

Have you been harboring your hurts? Are you ready to free yourself of that bitter spirit? If so, would you pray this prayer?

> *Lord, forgive me for hanging on to this destructive sin that has been slowly destroying me. Set me free—renew a right spirit in me. Put a song in my heart, and by Your grace I'll start praising instead of pouting.*

Note:
1. Rabbi Kushner in *Parade Magazine* (date unknown).

How Can I Get Out of This Financial Mess?

Possessions weigh me down in life;
I never feel quite free.
I wonder if I own my things,
Or if my things own me.[1]

HOW do people get themselves into such a mess? In our counseling with people, we have heard of many problems that lead people into financial bondage. Some of their problems come suddenly as a result of losing a job, medical bills, divorce, and other family situations. However, most come from poor money management that results from not living on a budget. We try to teach people to "live in your box." That means you live within your budget, not beyond it. We are convinced wise money management starts with a monthly budget or some other regular check on how much you are spending compared to how much you are earning. If your outgo exceeds your income, you are living outside your box.

A budget is a spending plan to enable you to keep control of the material things God has placed at your disposal. We trust this lesson will teach you how to "live in your box." We want to share five keys to financial liberty.

Keys to Financial Liberty

A. Learn to Love God More than Your Money

1. What do people tend to do when they make a great deal of money? Read 1 Timothy 6:17.

2. God gives us many things to enjoy. How does He want us to feel about our material possessions? Read 1 John 2:15 and Matthew 6:24.

3. Read 1 Timothy 6:10. Why is God concerned that we not love our money and the things it can buy?

4. How can you tell if you love your money more than you love God? Read Matthew 6:24.

B. Learn to Be Content with What You Have

5. What would you say is one of the main causes for financial bondage? Read Hebrews 13:5 and 6.

6. Read Hebrews 13:5 and 6 and Philippians 4:11. How can we Christians be freed from the bondage of discontentment?

7. The world says, "He who dies with the most toys wins!" Read Luke 12:15–21. What does God say?

8. What riches do Christians have that money can't buy and that make them rich toward God?

From MY Perspective—Juanita

"I have learned, in whatsoever state I am, therewith to be content" (Philippians 4:11). Where was Paul when he wrote those words? In prison! He said he had learned to live on much and on little. Notice the key word in that verse is "learned." Due to our greedy, lustful, covetous sin nature, we are not naturally contented. However, with God's help and strength, we can learn to be content as He supplies our needs (Philippians 4:19). We can learn contentment faster if we don't get our "wanters" and our "needers" mixed up.

I recently read that Christian materialism is believing that happiness can be found in things rather than in Christ. It can be cured only when we choose to believe that our longings are met in Christ, not in material possessions. Are you content with God's provisions, or do you always want more? I have been on both sides of the track. There was a time in my life when I thought things could make me happier. I remember years ago getting a new couch I had wanted so much. After I got the couch, it was just another thing to clean and take care of. It couldn't change a thing in my heart. A couch cannot bring peace and happiness. I have learned that only the Lord brings joy that lasts.

Learning to be content with God's provisions will allow you to take a giant step toward financial liberty and enable you to enjoy the true riches of life. One wise person said it this way: "Discontentment makes rich people poor. Contentment makes poor people rich." Which side of the track are you on?

C. Be Aware of Satan's Trap

9. Living in this materialistic age can be dangerous to our spiritual health. Read Deuteronomy 6:10–15 and 8:10–20. What are two tendencies that often follow financial prosperity among believers?

10. Read Matthew 6:24–34. When Christians begin to live for money instead of God, Satan has them where he wants them. They soon will be in bondage to their possessions. What will free them from this bondage?

11. Read Philippians 4:15–19. What is involved in trusting God to meet our financial needs?

D. Have a Plan to Get out of Debt

Are you telling your dollars where to go, or are you continually asking, "Where have they gone?"

Listed below are some warning signs credit managers give as indications that a person is headed for financial trouble.

- At least 20 percent or more of his or her income is needed to pay accumulated debts.
- His debt keeps getting higher because he adds new ones before paying off the others.
- She is stretching her debts to have a longer time to pay them off.
- He often has unpaid bills and can't seem to get everything paid each month.

12. Most families do not get into financial problems because they earn too little. Read Matthew 6:25–33. What common problem do many people have?

13. Would you like to get yourself out of your financial mess? If so, you must create a plan to accomplish this desire. Do you believe it can happen? See Luke 18:27 and Philippians 4:13.

From MY Perspective—J. O.

Cancer is one of the most dreaded diseases. We know that often it can mean a slow death. If we feared materialism as much as we fear cancer, we would avoid most of our financial problems. Materialism is a potentially fatal disease for our spiritual life. The dictionary defines "materialism" as "the tendency to be more concerned with material than with spiritual values."

Someone said that Americans spend money they don't have on things they don't need to impress people they don't like. In America, with the constant pull of materialism on all of us, the test of our character is how we spend our money. Christ says that either money will control our lives or He will control our lives—we must make the choice: "No man can serve two masters: for either he will hate the one, and love the other; or else he will hold to the one, and despise the other. Ye cannot serve God and [money]" (Matthew 6:24). We are slaves either to God or to money. I have chosen to be a slave to God. What choice have you made?

Suggested Plan to Eliminate Accumulated Debts

• List all the debts that need to be eliminated. (Do not include your house and car payments.)

• Set a realistic goal of when you want to have your debts paid off (12–48 months, for example). You may need to talk to your creditors and ask them to work with you to pay off your debts. Some credit card companies will lower your interest if you explain your circumstances and your plan to pay off your debts.

• Do not make any new credit purchases until you have paid off your present debts.

• Double your payments or start a savings plan as your debts decrease.

• Sell any unnecessary items to help pay off your debts.

• Get a part-time job, if possible, until your debts are paid.

• Ask for God's help each day in disciplining your desires.

• Don't give up—stick to your plan!

E. Learn to Live on a Budget

14. Memorize 1 Timothy 6:8 and Hebrews 13:5 and meditate on them often. How can these verses help you know the difference between a need and a want?

15. Are you "living in your box"? To find out, write down your monthly income and outgo. If your outgo exceeds your income, you are living on more than you make—you are outside your box.

Suggested Tips to Set Up a Budget

Give 10 percent to the Lord's work.
Save 10 percent (if possible) or $10 a month.
Live on the other 80 percent.

From MY Perspective—Juanita

The Old Testament mentions giving a tithe (10 percent) of one's income. The New Testament simply tells us to give liberally (2 Corinthians 9:6, 7). If a tithe was required under the Mosaic law, we would surely want to give even more, if possible.

Many years ago one of God's faithful servants challenged us to give 10 percent for one year. He told us that if God didn't richly bless us for our giving, he would personally give us back everything we gave. God met all of our needs and some of our "greeds." Since that time, 10 percent comes out of our check first. Over the years God has allowed us to increase our giving beyond the 10 percent for the support of missionaries around the world.

"No one can serve two masters." Either God will be first in our money, time, and talents, or the things of this world will have top priority. Have you been trying to straddle the fence? Have you been trying to serve two masters? We must remember that all our possessions are on loan to us from God. We can either squander them on earthly things or invest them in eternal things with eternal rewards. The choice is ours!

16. In Genesis 41:25–27 Joseph interpreted a dream for Pharaoh. He told the king there would be seven years of prosperity followed by seven years of famine. In verses 34–36 Joseph gave Pharaoh a plan that would enable him to handle the problem. What did Joseph tell the king to do?

17. What principle was he teaching that wise men live by today?

From MY Perspective—J. O.

"A penny saved is a penny earned." Let your money work for you, not against you. If you save 10 percent of your check each month, you probably will never have financial problems. "But," you might be thinking, "I do have financial problems, and I can't save 10 percent a month." But could you save $10 a month after all? Everyone could save $2.50 a week by skipping something like a trip to McDonald's one time. Have you ever figured out what $10 a month could add up to in thirty-five years? Bruce Peterson did in his book *Total Life Management.* Below are the results of his calculations:

$$\begin{array}{r} \$10 \text{ a month } = \ \$120 \text{ a year} \\ \underline{\times 35} \\ \$4,200 \end{array}$$

If you saved $10 for thirty-five years at 5 percent interest, you would have more than $11,000; at 10 percent, more than $33,000; at 15 percent, $105,000.

Will you start saving at least $10 a month, or will you be the one pictured in Proverbs 21:20: "There is treasure to be desired and oil in the dwelling of the wise; but a foolish man spendeth it up"?

Write down your monthly income. . . . . _____

List your monthly expenses.

    Offerings to the Lord's work . . . . _____

    Savings . . . . _____

    Food . . . . _____

    House payment . . . . _____

    Car payment . . . . _____

    Utilities and other household expenses . . _____

    Transportation . . . . _____

    Personal allowances . . . . _____

    Miscellaneous . . . . _____

    Insurance premiums (save a portion
      each month so you have the money
      when the bill comes) . . . . _____

    Medical . . . . _____

    Clothing . . . . _____

    Eating out and recreation . . . . _____

    Education bills . . . . _____

    Credit cards . . . . _____

Are you "living in your box"? If you cannot pay your credit card off in thirty days, you are living outside your box!

Are you tired of being in financial bondage? Will you start applying these "keys to financial liberty" to your life so you can be set free?

    A. Love God more than your money.

    B. Learn to be content with what you have.

    C. Be aware of Satan's trap.

    D. Have a plan to get out of debt.

    E. Learn to live on a budget.

From YOUR Perspective

Has materialism been draining your spiritual life? Have you gotten your priorities out of order, and God is no longer first in your life? If so, would you pray this prayer?

Lord, free me from the bondage of materialism. Too much of my life has been centered around comfort and belongings. Give me the courage to let go of my desire for more things. Help me to put You first in my life with my giving, time, tastes, and talent.

Note:
1. Author unknown.

Why Must I Forgive When I Did Nothing Wrong?

MOST of the ground Satan gains in our lives comes from an unforgiving spirit. We are warned to forgive others so that Satan can't take advantage of us (2 Corinthians 2:10, 11). God requires forgiveness, or He will turn us over to the tormentors (Matthew 18:34, 35). When we won't forgive, we are tormented with feelings of guilt, anger, hatred, and revenge. Forgiveness is hard, and it will hurt, but it will also heal. No matter how bad the hurt may be, it will be easier to forgive than live with the open wound you now bear if you are living with an unforgiving spirit. We are to be merciful, just as our Heavenly Father is merciful (Luke 6:36). We are to forgive as we have been forgiven (Ephesians 4:31, 32).

Before we start this lesson, we must settle in our minds that God expects us to forgive others the same way He forgives us. We will never know the freedom of forgiveness until we do it God's way. God's forgiveness toward us is both positional and parental, conditional and unconditional.

God's Positional Forgiveness

When we are born again, our sins—past, present, and future—are forgiven. Positionally God sees us justified, or just as if we had never sinned (Romans 3:21–24). *The fact of our for-*

giveness is settled forever. Jeremiah 31:34 states, "I will remember their sin no more."

God's Parental Forgiveness

Although we have been forgiven eternally, we still sin. When we sin, we lose intimacy with our loving Heavenly Father. We do not lose our salvation, but we do lose our fellowship. David illustrated this truth in Psalm 51:12–14, where he wrote, "Restore unto me the joy of thy salvation." *The joy of our forgiveness is secured daily.* First John 1:9 tells us that "if we confess our sins, he is faithful and just to forgive us our sins."

God's Unconditional Forgiveness

God's forgiveness is unconditional. He continues to forgive us whether we ask or not (Colossians 3:13; Ephesians 4:32). *Our forgiveness must be unconditional.* When we know we have not forgiven someone, we must forgive whether that person asks for forgiveness or not. Otherwise, we will short-circuit our fellowship with the Lord (Mark 11:25, 26).

God's Conditional Forgiveness

When we have known sin in our lives, it breaks our fellowship with the Father, but He forgives when we confess (1 John 1:9). *Our forgiveness must be conditonal.* When fellowship has been broken, it cannot be restored until the offender confesses his sin and asks for forgiveness. Only then can forgiveness that restores fellowship be given. See Luke 17:3.

Have you have been in bondage to another person because of an unforgiving spirit? Our prayer is that you will know the freedom of forgiveness after studying this lesson.

1. What is forgiveness?

2. Is forgiving the same as forgetting? Explain your answer.

3. Someone has said, "Life is like a boomerang—what you throw out is what you get back." How does this saying relate to Luke 6:38?

4. How do you explain Matthew 6:14 and 15 and Mark 11:25 and 26?

5. How does God view an unforgiving spirit?

6. Read Psalm 66:18. What happens when we "regard iniquity," including lack of forgiveness?

7. When we have an unforgiving spirit, what happens to us? See Luke 15:28.

From MY Perspective—J. O.

We must daily be forgiving the small offenses against us. Why? Learning to forgive in small things will teach us to more easily forgive when the large offenses come. If we can forgive the small offenses, we will be prepared for those adversities that tend to rip our hearts open and make us want to fight back.

Forgiveness is a lifelong process of learning and relearning, because no two experiences are ever exactly alike. I am not an expert on forgiveness, because this is one area in which practice does not make perfect. But I am learning to do it more quickly. I have learned by experience that an unforgiving spirit is a dead-weight that slows me down. I have too many other things to do with my life than to let myself get bogged down with unforgiveness.

I read of a young man who had been in prison for two years, and he wanted to return home. He had had no contact with his parents during those years. Three weeks before his release, he wrote his parents and told them how sorry he was that he had disappointed them. He asked them to forgive him. He said he would understand if they couldn't forgive him. He suggested that they tie a white ribbon on the old apple tree in the front yard if they wanted him. If he didn't see a ribbon, he wouldn't get off the bus and would move on. As the bus neared his house, he was afraid to look out the window for fear of being disappointed. But when he looked, the entire tree was covered with white ribbons. Are you as willing to forgive others as God is willing to forgive you?

8. To restore fellowship with God, we must confess our sin. To restore fellowship with someone with whom we have had a problem, what must we do? Read Matthew 5:23 and 24.

9. Jesus gave us an example of the forgiveness process in Luke 17:3–5. Does this passage mean that we must rebuke someone every time he or she hurts our feelings? If not, what does the passage mean? Read 1 Peter 4:8 as well.

10. What does it mean to rebuke a person?

11. How should we confront? Read Ephesians 4:15 and 32 and
    Colossians 3:12–14.

From MY Perspective—Juanita

If you are like me, confronting other people is something
you avoid. Yet Christ tells us we must do this if fellowship is to
be restored. To keep my fellowship with God, I must forgive
others in my heart whether they ask for forgiveness or not.
However, to restore fellowship with them I must confront their
sin. I must tell them how they have hurt me. Why? To hold a
person accountable for his actions shows him I value our relationship. People may continue committing the same offense until someone loves them enough to challenge their actions. What
happens if you confront them but they will not confess their sin
and ask your forgiveness? You must then tell God you forgive
them, but you cannot tell those people that you forgive them
until they ask for forgiveness. There would be no point in telling
them you forgive them when they will not admit they have done
anything wrong.

If you feel you must rebuke or confront someone who has
hurt you, make sure you check your attitude before you speak.
Be sure you "speak the truth in love."

12. Luke 17:3 states that you are to forgive if the person you
    rebuke repents. Is just saying, "I am sorry" repentance? Why
    or why not? What does it mean to repent?

13. How did the prodigal son in Luke 15:11–24 picture true repentance?

14. How does the father picture for us true forgiveness? Read Luke 15:20–24.

15. Look at the difference in the attitude of the forgiving father and the unforgiving older brother. Read Luke 15:25–32.

   The father was full of joy and _____ (v. 32).

   The son was full of _____ and jealousy (vv. 28–30).

16. Why is forgiveness described as a lifelong process? Read Luke 17:3 and 4 and Matthew 18:22.

17. Read Luke 17:5. How did the apostles feel after Christ told them to forgive seven times in one day?

From MY Perspective—J. O.

   Forgiving seven times in one day, or "seventy times seven," seems impossible. Yet Christ commands us to forgive others the same way He forgives us. "Even as Christ forgave you, so also do ye" (Colossians 3:13).

Donald Grey Barnhouse, a well-known preacher, told the story of a person who had lived a wild, reckless life. Later he was saved, and he married a wonderful Christian woman. One day the man told his wife of his past life of sin. She hugged him and told him she knew he was thoroughly converted but that he still had a sin nature. She explained to him, "I am sure Satan will do everything he can to pull you back into sin and cause you to fall. If this should happen, Satan will tell you there is no use trying again. He will also tell you not to tell me, since the news would crush me." Then she said an astonishing thing: "I want you to know that here in my arms is your home." She went on to say that when she married him, she married his old and new nature. She wanted him to know, in advance, that there was full pardon and forgiveness for any sin that might come into his life.

This story is a beautiful picture of God's relationship to us.

18. In what way do we often act like the unmerciful servant in Matthew 18:21–35?

19. Whom do you need to forgive? Whom do you need to confront? When are you going to do it? Will you do it now? Will you forgive even if the other person will not confess his or her sin?

Make a list of all those who have offended you. Decide that you will bear the burden of their offenses by not using any information you have against them in the future. Don't wait until you feel like forgiving; you will never get there. For each person on your list, say, "Lord, I forgive [name] for [offenses]." Positive feelings will eventually follow; freeing yourself from the past is the critical issue for now.

From MY Perspective—Juanita

I once read of a lady who had lived a sinful life as a youth and often said she could never forgive herself even though she had repeatedly confessed her sin to God. What was the problem? Someone in her past had abused her. She had never forgiven him. Because of her failure to forgive the man, the sins of her youth had pierced her heart for years. She could not accept God's forgiveness for her youthful sin. Instead, she was tormented by feelings of guilt. She continued to feel guilt until she was willing to forgive her offender.

"If ye forgive not men their trespasses, neither will your Father forgive your trespasses" (Matthew 6:15). If we want to know God's forgiveness, we must forgive. As we accept God's forgiveness (1 John 1:9) and forgive others as God commands, we are released from the feelings of guilt and torment (Matthew 18:34, 35).

From YOUR Perspective

Are you still in bondage to another person because of an unforgiving spirit? Would you like to be set free? If so, would you pray this prayer?

> *Lord, I'm tired of being in bondage to these people whom I have not forgiven. I now forgive them. Please set me free! I want to feel the freedom of forgiveness. I transfer whatever judgment they deserve into Your hands. I know You will mete out the justice deserved. I want to be relieved of the burden of holding them in my prison. Help me to keep forgiving the same way You keep forgiving me.*

L E S S O N   N I N E

How Can I Shed the "I Can't" Complex?

GOD often puts us in situations that look impossible or too hard so that He can show us that no situation is too hard for Him. One of our greatest sins is facing human problems with our weak, human resources. We often say to others or to ourselves, "It can't be done! It won't ever happen!" Yet God asks, "Is any thing too hard for the LORD?" (Genesis 18:14; cf. Jeremiah 32:17).

"With God nothing shall be impossible" (Luke 1:37). This statement was made by the angel after God told a young lady named Mary that she would have a child. Nothing is unusual about the announcement that she was questioning—except that she had never had a relationship with a man. How did she react? "It can't be done"? "This is impossible"? No; she instead asked, "How will it be done?" (See Luke 1:34.)

Do you face the future with optimism, knowing nothing is too hard for the Lord? Or do you face it with overwhelming doubt and fear, wondering how you are going to make it? Is your life characterized by faith or fear? If you are a negative thinker, you may have an "I can't" complex you need to shed. We desire to help you make that change as you study this lesson.

A Picture of the "I Can't" Complex

1. How would you describe an "I can't" complex?

2. Read Numbers 13:25–33. What negative things were the ten spies looking at?

Numbers 13:31—

Numbers 13:33—

3. Read Numbers 14:1–3. What did the Children of Israel look at?

4. What did their "I can't" complex foster in their hearts? See Numbers 14:8–10.

5. Read Numbers 14:20–23. What was the result of their unbelief?

From MY Perspective—J. O.

Twelve spies went into the land of Canaan to survey the territory God had promised them. Two came back ready to conquer the land: "Let us go up at once, and possess it." Ten had a negative report: "We [are] not able to go up against the people; for they are stronger." The ten men saw giants, but Caleb and Joshua saw God. The ten spies had a defeatist attitude. They thought, "We can't do it; we'll fail. We look like grasshoppers next to the giants."

When we have a negative "I can't" spirit, we'll see ourselves as helpless grasshoppers, and nothing anyone else can say will help us. Why? Because our mind-set is to face human problems with human resources. We will always see the giants instead of God. What giant problems do you have? If you do not overcome your problems, they will eat you up with fear and despair, as they did the ten spies: "[It] is a land that eateth up the inhabitants thereof" (Numbers 13:32).

Instead of letting our problems eat us up, we must quit retreating and march forward with God to "eat up" our problems. That's what Joshua and Caleb wanted to do: "Neither fear ye the people of the land; for they are bread for us" (Numbers 14:9). They saw the giants as "food" to make them stronger. They felt they would be stronger by overcoming the giants than if they had had no giants to overcome. The apostle Paul felt the same way when he wrote, "Therefore I take pleasure in infirmities, in reproaches, in necessities, in persecutions, in distresses for Christ's sake: for when I am weak, then am I strong" (2 Corinthians 12:10). When we run out of strength, that's when God's supernatural strength can work in us.

Have you been facing human problems with human resources? Start dwelling on God's greatness instead of your weakness. See yourself as a giant instead of a grasshopper!

6. God was angry with His children because of their unbelief. Notice what God stated in Numbers 14:11: "And the LORD said unto Moses, How long will this people provoke me? and how long will it be ere they believe me, for all the signs which I have shewed among them?" God had proved to them time after time that His hand was upon them. What were some of the miraculous signs they had seen? Read the verses below and record the miraculous signs.

Exodus 13:21—

Exodus 14:13–16—

Exodus 16:4—

Exodus 17:1–7—

7. Just as God was angry with the Children of Israel because of their unbelief, surely we must provoke Him with our unbelief as well. God planned for His children a land and a life flowing with milk and honey (Numbers 14:8), yet many of them never experienced it. What kind of life has God planned for believers today? Read John 10:10 and 15:11.

8. Read Hebrews 3:7–19. Why do so few Christians experience the life God planned for them?

9. Do you have any "giants" in your life? If so, how have you been viewing your situation?

From MY Perspective—Juanita

Have you learned that God often puts "giants" in our lives to teach us valuable lessons? What did David learn when he faced a giant? He clearly understood that if God did not deliver him, he would die: "I come to thee in the name of the LORD of hosts. . . . The battle is the LORD's" (1 Samuel 17:45, 47).

God often puts us into situations that are beyond our capabilities to teach us that nothing lies beyond His capabilities. What an exciting lesson to experience and learn! Is a giant in your life filling you with fear? Will you turn loose of this fear and give it to the Lord? Do you believe nothing is too hard for God to handle (Jeremiah 32:17)? Alexander MacLaren has some good advice for you: "Let us move on and step out boldly, though it be into the night where one can scarcely see the way. . . . There are things God gives us to do without any light or illumination at all, except His own command, but those who know the way to God can find it in the dark." Don't doubt in the dark what you know in the light!

10. Let's look at a few people who had giants in their lives.
Look up the following verses. Identify the person and the
way that person viewed his or her situation.

Exodus 4:10–12—

Genesis 17:17—

Daniel 2:10–16—

1 Kings 17:8–12—

John 6:1–7—

11. How did these men and the woman conquer their difficult
situations?

Moses (Exodus 4:11–19)—

Abraham (Genesis 15:6)—

Daniel (Daniel 2:16–23)—

The widow at Zarephath (1 Kings 17:13–16)—

Philip (John 6:8–14)—

12. Each of these five Bible characters modeled an activity that we should make part of our lives. How will you apply that activity to yourself?

Moses modeled *obedience*.

Abraham lived by *faith*.

Daniel practiced *prayer*.

The widow demonstrated *submission*.

Philip learned by *giving*.

From MY Perspective—J. O.

I'm sure you could be thinking, "Those events are exciting to read about in the Bible. It's fascinating to read about how the widow's meal never ran out and how Christ fed five thousand people with one boy's lunch. But what about *me?* Where am *I* going to get enough money to pay *my* bills?"

We are so much like the woman at the well. Christ told her He wanted to give her living water, and she wanted to know how He could do it: "The woman saith unto him, Sir, thou hast nothing to draw with, and the well is deep: from whence then hast thou that living water?" (John 4:11). Christ promises to supply all our needs (Philippians 4:19). We counter, "Lord, I know You can do it, but I don't think You will." We just won't believe the promises of God. "But let him ask in faith, nothing wavering. For he that wavereth is like a wave of the sea driven with the wind and tossed. For let not that man think that he shall receive any thing of the Lord" (James 1:6, 7).

Will you start believing God, or will you continue to be tossed by your doubts and fears, never having your needs met as the Lord intends?

Steps in Shedding the "I Can't" Complex

STEP ONE: See God in Every Circumstance

13. How could 1 Corinthians 1:5 help you see God at work in everything?

STEP TWO: Shed the Loser's Limp

14. How would you describe a person with the "loser's limp"?

STEP THREE: Decide a Difficulty You Need to Conquer

15. Do you have a difficulty you need to conquer? If so, what is it?

16. How can you conquer your difficulty? Read John 15:5 and Philippians 4:13.

STEP FOUR: Use Your Failures as a Tool to Help Others

17. How can your past failures be an encouragement to someone else? See 2 Corinthians 1:4.

From MY Perspective—Juanita

After you have finally shed the "I can't" complex, the day will come when you can tell someone else how your life used to be filled with doubts and fears. The Bible does not gloss over the doubts and fears of men and women whom we would call "giants of the faith." God reveals the good and the bad about these people. Great and honest people today do the same when they write their autobiographies. They include their dark side, their weaknesses. Why? Because we are helped when we know that others have struggled with the same weaknesses we have. We are encouraged when we read that they are now victorious overcomers, instead of victims who are overcome. We all can be overcomers just as God planned for us to be: "Nay, in all these things we are more than conquerors through him that loved us" (Romans 8:37).

From YOUR Perspective

Which will it be for you? Will you be a victorious overcomer or a victim who is overcome? Are you ready to shed the "I can't" complex?

If you have had a negative "I can't, God can't" spirit, will you pray this prayer?

> *Lord, forgive me for trying to face my human problems with my weak, human resources, when Your supernatural power is available for me. Help me to view my impossibilities with eyes of faith that say, "With God nothing shall be impossible!"*

Will I Always Feel This Lonely?

HOW could people be lonely in such a crowded, busy world? Easy! All this busyness adds to the problem of loneliness. People do not have to be alone to feel lonely. People can feel lonely in a crowded church pew, at an office full of people, or even at home with their own families.

What is loneliness? The dictionary defines it as "alone, isolated, unhappy at being alone, longing for friends." One university student asked, "Why am I so lonely when there are two thousand students here?" John Milton once said, "Loneliness is the first thing which God's eyes named as not good." (See Genesis 2:18.) What is causing this universal malady of loneliness?

Does your loneliness result from divorce, death of a spouse, or unemployment? Maybe loneliness is not a problem in your life, but we are sure you know someone who is struggling with this problem. Wouldn't you love to be an encouragement to that person?

In this lesson you will find some practical steps in identifying the causes of loneliness and how to deal with the unhappy results of a lack of intimacy. We certainly do not have all the answers, but we trust the Biblical and practical guidelines in this lesson will help you in learning to manage loneliness.

Loneliness

1. "Loneliness" has been termed the most desolate word in the English language. Why?

2. After you have read the following verses, what experiences would you say are most likely to produce acute loneliness?

Isaiah 6:1—

Deuteronomy 24:3—

Genesis 12:1—

3. What are some of the side effects of loneliness?

4. When God created man, He knew man would need companionship. How did God care for that need? Read Genesis 2:18, 21, and 22.

5. Read Psalm 42:1 and 1 Samuel 20:17. What twofold need resides in every human God created?

6. Augustine once said, "God created man for Himself, and our hearts are restless until they find rest in Him." Why is a relationship with God the greatest need in a lonely person's heart? See Luke 4:18.

From MY Perspective—Juanita

An American newspaper took a survey in an effort to determine what problems gave its readers the most concern. These problems, listed here in the order of priority, were the most prevalent in the responses: fear, worry, and loneliness. One writer said he thought loneliness casts the longest shadow on our contemporary world.

In another poll taken among patients at a psychiatric hospital, nearly 80 percent of the patients said loneliness caused them to seek psychiatric help. Surely loneliness is a pervasive condition. Most songs and movies feature broken relationships, infidelity, death, or desertion.

How different the life of the believer should be! Even in times of great loss and loneliness, we are never really alone. When we walk with Christ, He has promised never to leave us or forsake us (Hebrews 13:5). We should never feel lonely or lost. He saved us not only from our sins but also from a life of emptiness.

The Difference between Loneliness and Solitude

7. Read Mark 6:31 for a picture of solitude and 1 Kings 19:1–5 for a picture of loneliness. What is the difference between loneliness and solitude?

8. Sometimes we get so caught up in living, we forget to stop long enough to make a life. Why must we daily separate ourselves from others for a time of solitude with God? Read Psalm 46:10.

9. According to Isaiah 40:31, if we have times of solitude with God each day, what will they do for us?

From MY Perspective—J. O.

Times of solitude are very important in this hectic rat race of modern life. All of us have wished for hours of solitude now and then. In *Facing Loneliness,* Mumei said it like this:

> *I wish*
> *That I could enter in*
> *And close the door*
> *Of my small house*
> *To dwell alone*
> *As little shellfish do.*

Solitude is good because it is something we choose. Loneliness is not good because it occurs when others are separate from us, either by death or through other circumstances.

Christ was willing to experience loneliness in the Garden and on the cross so that He could know how we feel when we walk through the valley of loneliness. His disciples deserted Him in His hour of greatest need. Yet in that dark time of loneliness, He was not alone. He felt the Father's presence with Him after the disciples deserted Him: "Behold, the hour cometh, yea, is now come, that ye shall be scattered, every man to his own, and shall leave me alone: and yet I am not alone, because the Father is with me" (John 16:32).

God is just as close to us today as He was to His Son in the Garden. But if we do not believe this wonderful truth, it will be of no value to us; nor will we enjoy the benefit of His presence with us.

10. In Genesis 32:24–29 we see Jacob alone with God. What resulted from this lonely time in Jacob's life?

11. Think of the loneliest moment you have ever experienced. Did you feel totally alone, or did you sense God's presence with you?

Can you see a transforming effect in your life as a result of that lonely time?

12. A chronic illness, disease, or handicap can make a person feel imprisoned in a bed or wheelchair. How could that person's situation be transformed into a place of solitude and peace instead of a prison of loneliness? Read Isaiah 45:7 and Isaiah 26:5.

Causes for Loneliness

Bereavement

13. If you have lost a mate or loved one in death, describe how you felt those first few months.

From MY Perspective—Juanita

How can we help widows and widowers? We may not be able to help ease the pain in their hearts, but we can help ease the sense of loneliness. After my father died, I stayed with my mother about three weeks to help her through those first lonely days. After I returned home, I tried to send her a card every couple of weeks for about a year to cheer her up a bit. Often the cards were funny to give her a laugh. One card especially remains in my mind. It said, "Sometimes life is like a roller-coaster—it makes you want to puke!" I also communicated with her weekly by phone.

Widows who do not have children close by especially need our help with little things we take for granted. Where do they get the car fixed? Who will trim the trees? Who will put on a new roof? Their husbands always did these things; they do not know where to go or whom to call.

One of my friends commented to me how much her church helped her when her husband died and she was left with two young sons to raise. I asked her to share some of her thoughts with us.

> *About two weeks after Greg died, my pastor and a deacon took me to lunch and asked about any special needs we had. They asked specifically about my financial needs and inquired if we were okay financially. . . . I guess one of the ways people can help is simply to say, "I want to do something for you; how can I help?" . . . Ask good questions like, "When are you the busiest? What is hardest to get done? What jobs do you need help with?" One young mother wanted to help me. I told her Thursdays were my busiest days. She made dinner every Thursday for several months. Each spring and fall someone on the church service committee calls me for a list of everything I need to have done. They schedule a Saturday morning and come to do everything. Usually ten to twelve men are here working.*

Her church has a bulletin insert that lists opportunities for service, such as car repair, carpentry, child care, painting, plumbing, transportation, yard work. If you fill out the insert, you are put on the service committee and asked to help as needs arise. What a good idea! Is your church doing something like this? If not, pass the idea on to your pastor.

14. We are told that time is a great healer, but is it the greatest healer? Why? Read 2 Corinthians 1:3 and 4 and Isaiah 61:1–3.

15. Why would it be wrong for a Christian to become so obsessed with his or her loss that he or she becomes overwhelmed with grief? See Psalm 18:30.

Singleness (Having Never Been Married)

16. Some people are single by choice, and others wish they were not single. The Bible doesn't view singleness as the worst thing that could happen to a person (1 Corinthians 7:1, 7, 8, 25–27; Matthew 19:12). What would be worse than being single? Read Proverbs 25:24.

Divorce

Many have said that losing a mate in divorce is worse than losing one in death. Death is final! The consequences of divorce may never end. Couples who file for divorce are usually so caught up in the emotional turmoil of their problems that they give little thought to the far-reaching consequences of the divorce. They will have many, many problems to deal with, and loneliness is one of them.

17. A divorcé (divorced man) or a divorcée (divorced woman) may lose his or her mate and children. What else may a divorced person experience to add to his or her loneliness? Read Job 19:14.

18. Along with loneliness, what other emotions may the divorcé or divorcée have to deal with?

19. What common emotion must a divorced person deal with to help ease the pain of loneliness? Read Matthew 6:14 and 15 and Mark 11:25.

Unemployment and Retirement

From MY Perspective—J. O.

Another cause for loneliness that we often overlook is unemployment. Today it is not uncommon for competent, highly qualified men and women to be out of a job overnight due to companies' downsizing. A man in his late forties expressed some of his feelings when he was terminated from his job: "I felt worthless to myself and to my family; my self-esteem was crushed. I wanted to withdraw from friends and family. I soon felt my self-confidence going when I found out the company wanted to replace me with a younger man."

Speaking from my own personal experience, another cause for loneliness is retirement. When I retired from the pastorate, after thirty-two years of being with staff and ministering to people almost every day, the feeling of loneliness was overwhelming. The feeling of not being productive and needed was difficult to handle.

My wife and I are learning to adjust to a new way of life. We tell people we have not retired—just changed gears. We are now involved in an itinerant ministry around the U.S.A. and overseas. In our new ministries we are meeting new people all the time, but I am still adjusting to feelings of loneliness that I never experienced in the pastorate.

20. How can Philippians 4:11 and 19 help the pain of loneliness for the unemployed and retired?

Leaving Family and Friends

21. Moving to another town, country, or even another home in the same town can cause loneliness. Going away to college and many other changes cause loneliness. Read Philippians 2:25. What is a lonely person's basic need?

22. Why is a companion or friend the most effective barrier against loneliness?

23. If a person is going to find any relief from loneliness, what must he or she do? Read Proverbs 18:24.

Ways a Lonely Person Can Make New Friends

(1) Attend a small group Bible study or Sunday School class.

(2) Do volunteer work at a nursing home or hospital.

(3) Invite people into his or her home for a meal.

(4) Attend a once-a-week craft class, computer class, or some other type of class or meeting.

(5) Become involved in a team sport, if age and health will allow it.

A Spouse's Advice for Living through the Loss of a Mate

• Don't withdraw. Let people know you desperately need them.

• Stay busy. Plan ahead. Do for others. Go places with others, even if you don't particularly want to.

• Get rid of your mate's clothes. Rearrange the furniture.

• Don't get upset if your children do not grieve as you do.

• Write thank-you notes to people who help you. Express how much you needed them and appreciate them.

• Have one friend with whom you can share your heart and be totally honest.

• Stay looking as nice as you can. Buy some new clothes if your budget will allow it.

- Don't panic about money. Get professional help if you need it.
- Read a lot.

From MY Perspective—Juanita

If loneliness is not handled and dealt with, it can lead a person into a vicious circle of self-pity. I once read that there are two kinds of centers for our lives—self or God. If a believer's life is not God-centered, then it will be self-centered. How can we move from a self-centered life to a God-centered life? We must forget the past and start focusing on a God-centered future (Philippians 3:13, 14). Then we can get our eyes off our circumstances and onto the Lord (Psalm 25:15).

What will a God-centered life allow us to do? We will be able to accept God's will for our lives: "In every thing give thanks: for this is *the will of God* in Christ Jesus concerning you" (1 Thessalonians 5:18; emphasis added). We must look at everything we experience as God's choice for our lives, that "this is the will of God." When we can accept God's appointments for our lives, we quit resenting them and start living a life of peace. "In acceptance lieth peace." Acceptance gives us a quiet confidence that God is in control—without the need to understand what He is doing or why He has done it.

The lonely person has only two choices: (1) the self-centered life that succumbs to loneliness and continues to suffer the consequences or (2) the God-centered life that rises above the loneliness and enjoys relief. Your relationship to God is of utmost importance in enjoying inner security. What are you doing to develop a God-centered life?

Precious Promises to Help You Rise Above Your Circumstances and Keep Your Eyes on the Lord
Psalm 23:1–6

God is *with me*. He is my shepherd (v. 1).

God is *beneath me*. He provides green pastures (v. 2).

God is *beside me*. He keeps me safe beside still waters (v. 2).

God is *behind me.* He says that goodness and mercy will follow me (v. 6).

God is *beyond me.* Heaven is waiting for me (v. 6).

Isaiah 41:10

Don't become discouraged; God will strengthen and help you.

Isaiah 43:2

Your problems will not destroy you unless you try to handle them in your own strength.

Isaiah 40:31

When you feel you just cannot go on, God can renew your strength to take the next step.

Loneliness can be caused by the loss of a mate, divorce, relocating, confinement (resulting from an illness or a disability), and even living with an unsaved mate. Do any of these circumstances relate to people who attend your church? How could you reach out to at least one of them in loving concern?

From YOUR Perspective

Has your loneliness caused you to get into that vicious circle of self-centeredness? If so, would you pray this prayer?

> *Lord, forgive me for getting my eyes off You and putting them on myself. I want to quit dwelling on the past and start focusing on a God-centered future. I want to accept my situation in life as Your appointment for me. I also want to strive to find new ways of overcoming my loneliness.*

Is There a Way out of Depression?

ANGER, despair, guilt, loneliness, fear, fatigue—what other word could be linked to this list of words? Depression! These emotions are often the cause or result of depression. Is there a way out of depression? From personal experience, and from practical experience in helping others, we can answer yes!

Depression is one of the most common emotional problems in our nation today. It is a particularly serious and debilitating disorder often described as an emotional shutdown. Depression is not a disease. Medical science admits that the causes of depression are still largely unknown. Organic malfunctions can trigger feelings of depression; however, most symptoms are the consequences of thinking and acting in an unbiblical manner. In this lesson we want to familiarize you with the symptoms and causes of depression, as well as give you a plan for recovery.

You may not need this lesson for yourself. You may never have been depressed, and you may have a hard time relating to those who are. If that's true and if you have a heart for hurting people, then you need this lesson.

People who are depressed need someone who cares about them and will be patient with them. We know God has an answer for every problem we will ever face, but we need wisdom to know how and when to use the Word with depressed people. Many times they need someone who will listen to them more than talk to them. Ask God to open your eyes to the needs of the depressed and give you an understanding heart to help them.

Who Becomes Depressed?

Poor communicators. They do not know how to share their heart and feelings with others. Most of their thoughts are turned inward.

Overworked people. They often feel as if they have too much to do. They have a hard time keeping their priorities in order.

Bored people. They feel as if they have nothing to do. Life seems blah and meaningless.

Successful people. They have reached all their goals and feel as if they have nothing left for which to strive. Life has lost its purpose.

People in drastic circumstances. Divorce, loss of physical abilities, job loss, loss of a relationship, death of a loved one, financial reverses, accidents, retirement, and interpersonal relationships are difficult circumstances that people can find themselves in.

1. List other types of people who may be prone to depression.

Causes of Depression

The most common root problem is a feeling of unresolved anger. The person continues to dwell on and brood over his or her hurt. The anger can turn to grudges that need to be released, forgiveness that needs to be granted, or vengeance that needs to be removed from the heart. The depressed person often knows what his problem is, but he decides to hang on to his hurts and digs himself deeper into his pit of despair and hopelessness. Happiness is a choice! After someone recognizes his problem, he must face it, trace it, and ease it! The alternative is to stay miserable.

2. From your perspective, what are other causes for depression?

3. What physical problems do men and women experience that can lead to depression?

Symptoms of Depression

Passiveness and loss of interest. Depressed people do not care if things get done or not. They feel down all the time. They are moving toward emotional deadness.

Pessimism. A person's vision moves from positive to negative. Everything looks dark. That person feels sad and cries often.

Hopelessness. Hopeless people think things will never be right again. They have tried counting their blessings, but nothing works.

Feelings of worthlessness. The depressed person often suffers guilt because he does not live up to others' expectations. He feels overwhelmed with his circumstances and can't get back on his feet.

Withdrawal. Depressed people talk less and brood more. They withdraw communication, and then they withdraw physically. They often stay in bed longer and do not want to be around other people.

Self-centeredness. The depressed person begins to dwell on his feelings only. He wraps protective layers around his heart to keep from getting hurt again.

Fatigue. Fatigue causes people to feel dried up spiritually and too tired to function properly.

Underindulgence or overindulgence. Those with the problem of depression may either undereat or drink or overeat or drink.

Poor concentration. Depressed people have a hard time thinking clearly and making decisions. They go through the motions of doing what they should in their religious and daily duties.

Suicidal tendencies. Continued unbiblical thoughts and actions can lead to suicide. The depressed person begins to detach himself from reality and dream of death and how wonderful it would be.

4. Are you experiencing any of these symptoms? Do you think you are depressed? How would you explain the difference between discouraged and depressed people?

Let's look at David, a Bible character who was at the point of depression. He had many of the symptoms of depression but was not completely hopeless. Let's identify his symptoms of depression. Read Psalms 42 and 43 to get a picture of a very discouraged man who was hanging onto the edge of the pit of depression.

5. What symptom of depression was David experiencing in Psalm 42:1 and 2?

6. How was he feeling?

From MY Perspective—Juanita

David was tired and drained, and he may have even felt dried up spiritually—he was thirsting for God. "As the hart panteth after the water brooks, so panteth my soul after thee, O God" (Psalm 42:1). An old saint of God remarked, "A drying well will often lead the spirit to the river that flows from the throne of God." If you feel drained physically and emotionally and dried up spiritually, you are in a good place to draw close to Christ. We can praise God for the famine in our lives if it drives us in utter helplessness back to Him.

We are so much like the fearful, faltering Children of Israel who wandered in the wilderness when they could have been enjoying the blessings of the Promised Land. We could have absolute satisfaction and relief in Jesus Christ; yet we resist, resent, waste time wandering, and stay hungry. When finally in desperation we are driven to Christ, we wonder why we waited so long. Yet if we never had any severe tests in our journey here below, we would never know what a wonderful Guide and Deliverer we have.

If you are in a dried-up, famine time in your life, let it drive you to your knees and closer to God!

7. David was feeling sad and was crying a great deal of the time. How did those around him add to his suffering? Read Psalm 42:3.

8. David seemed to be doing all the right things; he kept going through his religious duties. He said, "I pour out my soul in me." What might this comment picture? Read verse 4.

9. What other question that he might have wanted to ask God could have crossed David's mind?

10. David was doing some self-talk in verse 5. What was he saying to himself?

11. Why was this kind of self-talk good for him?

12. What was David trying to do in verse 6?

13. Why was this action good for him?

From MY Perspective—J. O.

"O my God, my soul is cast down within me: therefore will I remember thee" (Psalm 42:6). Who calls the Majesty in the heavens, the Creator of the ends of earth "my God"? Many times it is the soul who is cast down and full of turmoil. Often it takes these lonely, dark times to bring us closer to God. In our desperation we cry, "My God . . . I remember thee." Then we take our eyes off our difficult circumstances and start remembering how great and powerful our God is. We remember His lovingkindness in the past, the strength He gave us to keep going when all human strength was gone, His help to bear our burdens.

Do you need some things to remember to help you keep going? Remember that though you are weak, He is strong; though you are poor, He is rich; though you are unfaithful, He is faithful. Pleasant memories of the past are like a light to pierce through the dark haze to help light our present gloom. When you feel down and out, remember the blessings of the past and believe the sun will shine again. Don't doubt in the dark what you know in the light! God's power will keep God's promises.

14. How was David feeling in verse 7?

15. In the midst of his turmoil and confusion, what was David still hanging on to (v. 8)?

16. What caused David to feel downhearted, discouraged, and near the point of depression (vv. 9, 10)?

17. In verse 11 we find David talking to himself again. What did he add to his conversation with himself regarding his countenance?

18. How did David ever get into such a state of mind? Reread Psalms 42 and 43 and count the number of personal pronouns that relate to David.

19. What do all these "me's," "my's," and "I's" tell you?

20. There are fifty-two first-person personal pronouns (I, me, my, mine) in these two psalms. How many times are "God" or "Lord" or a pronoun referring to God (him, his, thee, thy, thou, who) mentioned?

21. What does this contrast tell you about David?

22. What key problem was causing David so much emotional turmoil?

From MY Perspective—Juanita

David was suffering with PMS. However, it was not the PMS we most commonly hear about today. David was suffering from Poor Me Syndrome; his focus was more inward than upward. However, he did not stay there long; he knew the secret to getting back on his feet again: "I shall yet praise him" (Psalms 42:5, 11; 43:5). David knew he had to get his eyes off himself and back onto the Lord. He had to get a song in his heart again, a song of praise and thanksgiving to God. David had learned to sing praises to God at all times, even in his darkest moments. In his despair he would call upon God; his praises, mingled with his cries of anguish, resulted in victory.

Do you know anyone with Poor Me Syndrome? The real problem occurs when a person has it not only once a month, but every day. To turn this syndrome around, the person must do what David did: get his or her eyes off self and onto the Lord. The person must start praising in the midst of tears. A life of habitual thankfulness and praise results in a victorious life full of joy.

Dealing with Depression

To defeat the Poor Me Syndrome that often leads to depression, you must make a conscious effort to think right and act right each day. To help you get started, we suggest you try this three-step plan for two weeks.

STEP ONE: Exercise

Exercise each day for twenty minutes, if possible. This activity will release endorphins that become depleted when you are depressed. If you have withdrawn from people, try to go outside your home to exercise.

STEP TWO: Think Right

Do one "think right" question each day for a week.

Day 1

Remind yourself that God has promised to take care of you in every circumstance in life, no matter how overwhelming it may seem. Read each passage or verse and then write how it helps your thinking.

Psalm 23—

Psalm 37:5—

Proverbs 3:25, 26—

Day 2

Confess all sinful and hurtful thoughts to God and ask for His help in changing your thought patterns. When you have confessed all known sin, you can be sure you are totally forgiven. Write down how these verses help your thinking.

1 John 1:9—

James 1:5—

Psalm 103:10–14—

Day 3

Center your thoughts on pleasing and glorifying God and being a blessing to others in every situation. Read each verse; then list specific ways you will start thinking of others instead of yourself.

1 Corinthians 10:31—

Philippians 2:3, 4—

1 Peter 4:8–10—

Day 4

Discipline your mind to think on things that please God. Pray for those who are unkind to you. Write how each of these verses helps your thinking.

Philippians 4:8—

Colossians 3:2—

Matthew 5:44—

Day 5

Meditate on psalms, hymns, and spiritual songs you have memorized. How do these verses help your thinking?

Ephesians 5:19, 20—

Colossians 3:16—

Day 6

Keep reminding yourself that when you fail to meet your responsibilities in a Biblical way, you will think demeaning thoughts about yourself and will experience guilt. Read the following verses; then write how they help your thinking.

Romans 7:18–24—

Psalm 32:3, 4—

Day 7

How has your thinking been this week? Better or worse? Explain your answer.

How do Psalm 139:23 and 24 help your thinking?

STEP THREE: Act Right

Answer one "act right" question each day for a week.

Our emotions can produce words and actions that are displeasing to us and to God. Our behavior then produces thinking that troubles us. First, we must get our thinking right. Proper behavior and settled emotions will then follow.

Day 1

Confess recent or past unconfessed sins to those whom you have not treated in a Biblical way. If you have failed to fulfill your responsibilities in your home or at work, confess this failure as sin and make any needed corrections. Read these verses and write how they will help your actions today.

James 4:17—

James 5:16—

Psalm 51:1–4—

Day 2

Quit talking about and dwelling on your present difficult situation. Instead, remind yourself and tell others of the goodness of God. Develop the therapy of thanksgiving. Read the following verses. How can they help your actions?

Philippians 2:14, 15—

1 Thessalonians 5:18—

Hebrews 13:15—

Day 3

Do not use words that tear down other people. Refrain from quarrels, gossip, and slander. Are there other changes you need to make—you are home too much, are gone too often, spend too much money? How will these verses help your actions?

Proverbs 10:18—

Ephesians 4:25, 26—

Colossians 4:6—

Day 4

Release all feelings of vengeance against others who have hurt you. Have you tried to put any of these verses into action in your life? How?

Romans 12:19—

1 Peter 2:1—

Colossians 3:8—

Day 5

If you have ill feelings toward or unresolved issues with another person, initiate reconciliation with him or her. Read the following verses. How will these verses help your actions?

Matthew 5:9—

Matthew 5:23, 24—

Romans 12:18—

Day 6

Forgive anyone with whom you cannot reconcile your differences. You must do this to have fellowship with God and to have your prayers answered. Read the verses below. Write how each verse helped you.

Ephesians 4:32—

Matthew 6:14, 15—

Colossians 3:13—

Day 7

Start living a Spirit-controlled life instead of a self-controlled, self-centered life. Begin by doing what you know God wants you to do, whether you feel like it or not. Feelings follow obedience, not the other way around. If you have been missing services at church, start attending every service and volunteer to help in some area where help is needed. How will these verses help you?

Ephesians 5:18–21—

Galatians 5:16–24—

James 4:17—

From MY Perspective—J. O.

David was passing through the dark valley of despondency. His soul was fixed on God, but his mind and body were feeling the awful effects of depression and despair. Have you been there? If not, you may pass through this valley someday. It seems God wanted to emphasize this common weakness of man, because Psalms 42 and 43 repeat the following words three times in 42:5 and 11 and 43:5: "Why art thou cast down, O my soul? and why art thou disquieted within me?" The only ray of light in David's darkness was his confidence that the Lord loved him and would help him.

When we feel down and despondent, we need to do what David did, that is, ask ourselves why. Why do I feel so down and discouraged? Why do I feel no rest or peace? Is my sin or someone else's sin troubling me? Are the misfortunes of life causing my turmoil? How did David get out of the pit of despair? He started talking to himself. He might have said something like this: "Soul, I want you to listen to me. You've been whining and moaning long enough. It hasn't solved anything. You've been down long enough. It is time for us to move on." Then he gave himself an order: "Hope thou in God: for I shall yet praise him, who is the health of my countenance, and my God" (Psalm 42:11).

Are you in the pit? Do you need to talk to yourself a little? Do you need to tell yourself to "hope in God"? If you will begin to look at the greatness of your God and remember all His attributes and abilities instead of your failures and troubles, you can begin to move upward. Remember, where there is a will, there is a way! By an act of your will and with the help of God, get up and move on.

From YOUR Perspective

Are you ready to make some changes in your life? If so, will you pray this prayer?

> *Lord, I have lost hope that things will ever change. Forgive me for not trusting You. I want to put my hope in You and believe that nothing is impossible with God (Luke 1:37). With Your help and strength I will start thinking and acting right!*

Are You a Winner, Loser, or Chooser?

IN this series of lessons we have tried to cover various subjects people in turmoil must deal with. Now the choice is yours. What will you do with all the things that you have learned? Will you choose to apply these truths to your life and be happy, or will you continue to wallow in self-pity and resentment? Remember, we are not winners or losers, but choosers. Will you choose happiness? You can have it, because happiness is a choice.

Are you convinced Christ is all you need for life and godliness (2 Peter 1:3)? Have you settled it in your heart that God is enough? When you finally learn that God is enough, you are on your way to finding the happiness we all long for in this life.

We have known Christ as our Savior for many, many years now, and He has not failed us once. We have never found a struggle for which God's Word did not have a promise or directive uniquely suited to help us face and conquer it. Truly we have learned and can sing "Christ Is All I Need."

Are you enjoying the benefits of happy, abundant living now and eternal life beyond the grave? If not, why not? If you follow the Biblical formula we have introduced to you, we can guarantee you both! They are yours for the taking. Wouldn't you like to step out of the cycle of stress, strain, and struggles and start enjoying the overflowing, abundant life God has planned for you?

Our formula for happiness has two simple phases:

Phase One: Eternal life—beyond the grave.
Phase Two: Abundant life—now!

Eternal Life

The abundant, happy life does not begin until we receive Christ as our Savior. If you have never known happiness, you may not have eternal life. Only when you know the Shepherd can you feel the security of the lost sheep He found and cares for. "My sheep hear my voice, and I know them, and they follow me: and I give unto them eternal life; and they shall never perish, neither shall any man pluck them out of my hand" (John 10:27, 28).

1. Do you have eternal life? Read each of the verses below and then write by each verse what proofs of eternal life will be evidenced in a believer's life.
1 Peter 2:2—

Psalm 119:105—

John 14:15—

Romans 8:14–16—

1 John 4:7, 8—

Matthew 6:14, 15—

2 Corinthians 5:17—

Did you pass the test? How many of the evidences of eternal life characterize your life? If you are not sure you have eternal life, why not make sure right now? Read the following verses and then express your desire to God in prayer.

John 3:16; 10:10—God **loves** you and wants you to enjoy the **abundant life** He offers you.

Romans 3:23; 6:23—Human beings are sinful, and their sin **separates** them from God.

Romans 5:8; John 14:6—Jesus Christ's death is the only **provision** God has made to pay for the sins of humankind.

John 1:12—You must **receive** Jesus Christ as your Savior before you can personally experience His love for you and the abundant life He has planned for you.

Ephesians 2:8, 9; Romans 10:13—You can invite Christ into your life right now by a simple act of **faith.**

2. Are you ready to invite Christ into your life to be your Savior? Use the following prayer to help you express your desire to God.

> *Lord Jesus, thank You for dying on the cross for my sins. Right now I open my heart and invite You into my life as my Savior. Thank You for forgiving my sin and giving me everlasting life. I want You to have control of my life so that I can experience the abundant life You have planned for me.*

The Bible promises **eternal life** to all who receive Christ as Savior (1 John 5:11–13).

From MY Perspective—Juanita

How long has it been since you rehearsed your salvation experience with someone? We need to do this occasionally to keep it alive and exciting in our minds. So, if you don't mind, I'll take a couple of minutes and share my experience with you.

It was a Sunday evening many, many years ago in a little country church in Mount Vernon, Illinois. I was with my boyfriend (who is now my husband). I went to church Sunday mornings, Sunday evenings, and Wednesday evenings, not so much to be in church but to be with my boyfriend.

On that Sunday evening we were sitting in the back of the church with the other teens. We were singing the closing song, and the pastor was inviting people to come forward to receive Christ. I saw J. O.'s father walking to the back of the church. This seemed unusual because he always sat on the front pew. I soon realized he was coming to talk to me. He asked me if I would like to get saved that night. Before I knew what was happening, I said yes and was walking to the front of the church. We got down on our knees by that front pew, and I invited Christ into my life to be my personal Savior.

Little did that teenager realize the abundant life God had in store for her. I wish I could tell you I started enjoying it immediately, but I didn't. I could have, but it took several years before I finally started to spend time in God's Word each day and daily surrendering my will to do God's will. It was then that I began to enjoy the abundant life God had in store for me.

Abundant Life

Christ planned for His children to live an abundant, happy life (John 10:10). Psalm 1 pictures for us the blessed, or happy, Christian and describes how he has this happy life.

Happiness

Happiness is not found in the world, but in the Word, the "law of the LORD."

3. Read Psalm 1:2. What do you think it means to "delight" in the Word of God?

4. How can a person find "delight" in reading the Bible? Read Psalm 1:2.

5. Based on Psalm 1:3, what four words describe the happy, fulfilled child of God?

Strength

6. The happy Christian is pictured as a strong tree. What is the significance of the tree's being planted by the "rivers of water"? Read John 7:37–39.

Do you draw your strength from Christ daily? Have you found Christ to be all you need for life and godliness?

Productiveness

7. As strong trees we are supposed to do more than stand around looking good. We are supposed to be productive. What kind of fruit should we be producing? Read Galatians 5:22 and 23.

8. Read Psalm 1:3. What do the words "bringeth forth his fruit in his season" indicate to you?

How much of the fruit of the Spirit is being displayed in your life each day? Have you found Christ is all you need to live the Spirit-controlled life?

Perseverance

Happy Christians are like evergreens. They are not green just in the spring; they keep growing and going. Psalm 1:3 says that their "leaf also shall not wither."

9. Describe the happy Christian whose leaves do not wither.

Do you display determination and consistency in your life? Have you found that Christ is all you need to keep growing and going?

Prosperity

10. If the happy Christian is living a fruitful, Spirit-controlled life, what kind of prosperity is he or she enjoying?

Do you feel rich because of your inward prosperity? Have you found Christ is all you need to be content and feel prosperous?

From MY Perspective—J. O.

Has contentment become a way of life for you? If it has, you are a prosperous person; you enjoy riches the world cannot buy. Because contentment is something you can't buy, it can be here today and gone tomorrow if you are not walking close to Christ each day.

Trying circumstances, more than anything else, can quickly rob us of contentment. When we allow our circumstances to victimize us, we lose our sense of peace and satisfaction. However, we can learn to be content in every situation in life, no matter how difficult it might be (Philippians 4:11). How is this contentment possible? We must learn to cast ourselves on the Lord's strength and say, "Lord, my human resources are not sufficient for this situation. I'm depending on You to see me through."

God's resources are like a pacemaker for the heart. A pacemaker kicks in when the heart it is attached to "doesn't work right." It is a sustaining power. When we come to the end of our resources, God's reservoir of spiritual power is like a pacemaker. It kicks in and gives us the strength to keep going. That's when Ephesians 3:20 becomes real to us; we can "do exceeding abundantly above all that we ask or think, according to the power that worketh in us."

You'll learn real contentment when you can't fix your marriage or your kids; when you're unable to fight the cancer that's eating up your body; when you can't solve your financial problems. That's when you'll turn to God to get the strength to keep going. That's when you finally learn what Paul meant when he concluded, "I have learned, in whatsoever state I am, therewith to be content" (Philippians 4:11).

11. What must a Christian do to have a happy, prosperous life filled with attitudes and actions that honor God? Where does such a life start, and how is it maintained? Read John 3:3–6 and Psalm 1:2 and 3.

12. Read Psalm 46:10. Many of us call daily Bible reading "daily devotions." What do you think it means when someone "goes through the motions" of devotions?

13. Are you building a closer relationship with Christ each day as you spend time in the Word, or are you just going through the motions of devotions? Describe your method of daily Bible reading.

From MY Perspective—Juanita

You may not know how to study your Bible to gain new truths from it each day. If this is the case, we have some suggestions for you. Here are just a few:

• If you want to read through your Bible in a year, read two chapters in the Old Testament and one in the New Testament each day. Choose a verse at the beginning of each week and memorize it throughout that week.

• If you use a daily devotional book, don't skip the suggested Scripture reading. Read several verses before and after the Scripture passage to get the context of the verse. Read the devotional thoughts and then record one verse from your reading that is especially meaningful to you. Write your verse in a daily journal and then write a prayer to the Lord about what the verse meant to you.

• If you would like to study a chapter each week, you might like this method. Ask yourself the following questions and record your thoughts in a notebook:

✓ Who is speaking? Who is spoken of? What would you say is the primary subject of the text? What is being said about the subject?

✓ When would I need to use this portion of Scripture?

✓ Why was this Scripture section written?

✓ What are some contrasts between the godly and ungodly?

✓ Does this chapter teach me anything about handling my problems?

✓ Does this portion of Scripture teach me anything about what God has done or will do?

✓ What attributes of God do I see in this portion of Scripture?

✓ What attributes do I need in my life?

✓ What am I going to do today to work on those attributes?

From MY Perspective—J. O.

Today's support and self-help programs for people appear good but often lead to a dead end with no permanent change in character and conduct. The shortcut to a permanent change in your attitude and actions starts with receiving the gift of eternal life and learning to live the abundant life. Remember, this abundant life is maintained by a daily direct line to Christ, reading and feeding in His Word.

Will you make a commitment to Christ to read your Bible and pray for the next thirty days? Why thirty days? Experts tell us that if we do anything for thirty days, it will become a habit.

If you will make this commitment, you will be on your way to the happy, abundant life. You will find that Christ is all you need for life and godliness.

From YOUR Perspective

Have you made sure you have eternal life? Are you living the abundant life God has planned for you? If you are ready to make a commitment to live the abundant life, you can pray the following prayer.

> *Lord, I want to live the abundant life You have planned for me. I have tried and failed so many times. This time I will do it with Your help and strength. I will not try to do it by self-discipline and determination. I will daily exchange my weak, puny strength for Your supernatural strength by reading and meditating on Your Word. I am making a commitment to You to read my Bible and pray for the next thirty days with the intent of developing this pattern as a daily practice in my life.*

A Word from the Authors

If God used this study to change your life in any significant way, would you write us and tell us about it? It is an encouragement for us to know if the material we are writing is practical and helpful to those who use it. You may write us at the following address:

J. O. and Juanita Purcell
5741 Hebron Lane
Lakeland, FL 33813

Leader's
Guide

Lesson 1

1. "Lord, take this out of my life; I cannot handle it any longer." *Have a few group members share their answers.*

2. God does what He chooses, when He chooses, without asking our permission. He has the right because He created everything and everyone.

3. Examples: You get a flat tire on the way to an important appointment; the air conditioner breaks down on the day out-of-town guests are arriving. *Have group members share some of their answers.*

4. Most people like to plan ahead and feel they have some control over their lives. *Have a few people in the group share their thoughts.*

5. Job.

6. He lost his cattle, his servants, and his children.

7. He had an attitude of trust. He blessed the name of the Lord and said, "The LORD gave, and the LORD hath taken away." He had a spirit of acceptance.

8. His body was covered with boils.

9. He had a spirit of acceptance. He asked his wife if they should accept good from God but not trouble.

10. They wrongly assumed that God causes people to suffer because of their sin (v. 6). Suffering is no more a sign of God's disfavor than continued prosperity is an indication of God's approval and blessing.

11. They encouraged Job to "get right with God." If Job would plead with God, they thought, surely He would make Job prosperous again (v. 6).

12. "Are you suggesting I challenge God? I cannot! Arguing with God would be useless. If I wanted to dispute with God, I would not be able to answer one out of a thousand of His questions. Who could resist God and come out ahead?" He still had a spirit of acceptance.

13. "Shew [show] me." These are the words of a discouraged, despondent man. When we hit bottom and feel abandoned, we feel God has forgotten us. We want to know if He is still there and why the situation is happening.

14. He called his friends miserable comforters.

15. He felt God was against him, that God hated him.

16. "Behold, I cry out of wrong." Lord, this is wrong! "There is no judgment [justice]." Lord, this is not fair!

17. "I would know the words which he would *answer me*, and understand what *he would say unto me*" (emphasis added).

18. We tend to say, "If you loved me, you would want to help me, or you would see it my way."

19. This reply is typical of children when they do not get their way: "If you loved me, you would let me do it."

20. *Job 38:4, 5*—Where were you when I laid the foundations of the earth and marked off its dimensions? God took Job on a whirl-wind nature hike to view all His creation. Then God reminded Job that He had made it all and that He has the right to govern it as well. *Job 38:12*—Have you ever told the sun when to rise and set. *Job 40:2*—Will the one who contends with the Almighty correct Him? *Job 40:8*—Would you discredit My justice or fairness? Would you condemn Me to justify your actions?

21. God wanted Job to know that He is the ruler and controller of this universe and that nothing could happen apart from His permission. It was as if God were asking, "Job, do you still think you know better than God what He should allow in your life? Remember, no one can tell God what to do. God is God, and you're not!" God wanted His holiness to move from Job's head to his heart.

22. Lord, I am so sorry for demanding answers from You. I did not understand that I do not need to know why. I could not put it all together, but now I understand that I don't need to know why. You are the judge, and You will do what is right.

Lesson 2

1. People can do things contrary to, and in defiance of, God's re-vealed will stated in His Word, but God never permits them to act contrary to His sovereign will.

2. We can make our plans, but they will succeed only when they are part of God's sovereign will for our lives.

3. That evil person's plans could be fulfilled only if God allowed them to happen.

4. *Matthew 10:29*—A sparrow cannot fall to the ground outside

His will. *John 19:10, 11*—The Roman soldiers could not crucify Christ unless God allowed the crucifixion.

5. God used the Chaldeans to correct His people for their good. Habakkuk was amazed that God would use a more wicked nation to punish Judah. The Babylonians did not know they were being used by God to help God's people return to Him. God often uses unusual "rods" to correct us.

6. He knows and orders every step we take; we are never out of His sight. We must never forget that He orders our steps and our stops.

7. Yes! However, we must remember His purpose is our ultimate good. That good is "to be conformed to the image of his Son" (v. 29). We are usually looking for immediate physical or material good. God's good purpose often takes time to develop in our lives.

8. God is always in control, even when things seem out of control from our perspective. Seeing God ruling in the universe—according to His good pleasure and permissive will for our lives—will change our perspective on life. It will save us many months, even years, of bitterness and discouragement.

9. No plan of God's can be stopped; when God acts, no one can change His actions, and no one can demand that He give an account of His actions. *Allow students to respond.*

10. *Allow group members to respond.* It should cause us to trust God even more when we realize He has a plan and purpose for our lives and has the power to accomplish His will. No person or circumstance can stop God's plan for our lives from being fulfilled.

11. To become more like Christ each day and live our lives to please God.

12. He wants us to be working for Him, while He keeps working on us to make us more like His Son.

13. God wants us to have hope for the future.

14. He said, "God sent me here. You meant it for evil, but God intended it for my good."

15. God is never the author of sin. God often judges people for the very sins He uses to carry out His purpose.

16. We will reap what we sow! David and Bathsheba are a good example of a sinful choice that reaped severe consequences.

17. God says, "[You thought] that I was altogether [like you]" (Psalm 50:21). We tend to think God will act and do things as we would. Yet we know His thoughts and ways are beyond our understanding. Some of His ways may never make sense to us.

Lesson 3

1. Purify them. Take out all the useless dross that would keep us from becoming gold vessels fit for His use.

2. It may not make sense to me, but it does to God. He knows what is going on because He has ordered it.

3. God not only knows your needs, but He has also promised to meet all your needs.

4. This verse reminds me of a chorus we sang years ago: "My Lord knows the way through the wilderness—All I have to do is follow." How true! When we seem to be lost in a dark wilderness of doubt and confusion, how comforting it is to be reminded that God still sees us. He knows exactly what is going on in our lives.

5. God wants to bless us and not harm us; He wants to give us a future full of hope.

6. (1) He wants us to learn to patiently endure and not give up when trials come. (2) God wants us to be "perfect," or spiritually mature. (3) He also wants us to be "entire," or complete. He doesn't want any missing pieces in our spiritual lives.

7. Patience, or perseverance, will develop experience, or character, in our lives. This character will develop hope, hope that God isn't finished with us yet; we are still under construction.

8. If God were unfair, then what He does would not be right. But He always does what is right. Life is not fair, but God is. God deals with us according to His fairness in mercy and faithfulness.

9. Life on this earth is as a vapor compared to our eternal life in Heaven. We can endure anything when we know it will not last forever.

10. I do not own my life, but God does. I do not have the right or the wisdom to choose my course in life. Why should I take on the awesome responsibility of trying to direct my life when God has promised to do it for me?

11. God takes all the good and bad things in our lives and fits them together for our spiritual good so that we might become like His Son, Jesus Christ.

12. *Have some group members share their experiences.*

13. *Have each person record his or her response, and then have a few people share their answers.*

14. *Encourage the class to answer honestly.*

15. *Have several group members share their answers.*

16. *Ask volunteers to share their answers.*

Lesson 4

1. It motivated greater trust in God and helped him meet a life-threatening emergency.

2. David was feeling down and discouraged. His stress was affecting him emotionally. He was crying a great deal and probably not eating much. "My tears have been my meat day and night" (v. 3). Stress is harmful when it is continual and there is no time for the body and mind to recuperate.

3. Martha was what some call Type A, and Mary was Type B. Martha was stressed, according to verses 40 and 41. She was cumbered, or careful, which means she was worried and troubled.

4. Lord, don't You care that my sister has let me do all the work? Tell her to help me.

5. *Have a few group members share their thoughts.*

6. Things. Martha was worried about many things. In our day those "things" to worry about could include that the meal might not be ready on time; the napkins might still need to be ironed and folded just right; the Jell-O might not come out of the mold; or, if it does, it might be runny. Martha needed help, and Mary was sitting, apparently relaxing, and listening to Jesus.

7. Time to slow down and spend time in God's presence.

8. Stress causes sleeplessnes. Sleeplessness causes us to be weary and feel fatigued.

9. They create strife and bitterness, as well as many other problems. These feelings increase a person's heart rate and elevate one's blood pressure.

10. It seems he didn't want to eat. Twice the Angel of the Lord said, "Eat." Elijah then went into the wilderness for forty days without eating.

11. Too much stress causes ulcers as a result of the extra acid flow in the system. Colitis can also occur as a result of the digestive system's being accelerated.

12. His body was apparently racked with pain, and he felt like an old man.

13. The head, neck, and back muscles become tense from the extra blood supply.

14. It causes shortness of breath due to the increase of oxygen in the blood.

15. He was overworked. He needed someone to share the load.

16. *Ask the group members to evaluate this area in their own lives.*

17. Conflicts with people.

18. *Ask the group members to evaluate this area in their own lives.*

19. He had committed adultery, and Bathsheba became pregnant.

20. *Ask the group members to evaluate this area in their own lives.*

21. He was running from God.

22. *Ask the group members to evaluate this area in their own lives.*

23. *Take a few minutes to have everyone do a self-exam.*

24. Our bodies are the temple of the Holy Spirit; they belong not to us but to God.

25. Exercise relaxes the muscles made tense and tight from stress, and it increases the endurance of the body's cardiovascular and pulmonary system.

26. We find ourselves eating fast food rather than cooking healthful, nutritious food. When we don't eat properly, we're conforming to the world's standard of putting convenience above health.

27. Rest and relax.

28. *Ask for student responses.*

29. The man who tries to live his life in his own strength and does not need God is cursed. He will live a lonely life and won't see good when it comes.

30. The man who trusts God and puts his confidence in Him. His roots are firmly planted in God's Word; and when the trials come, he endures them and grows from them—he doesn't wither up and die.

Psalm 1:1–3 is also a good picture of the blessed person.

Lesson 5

1. The shepherd knows the best place for his sheep to graze and the location of water to quench their thirst. The sheep depend totally on the shepherd for their management and care.

2. He has planned for His sheep eternal life with Him in Heaven. While I wait for Heaven, He plans for me to live an abundant life here on earth, free from burdens and worries. He wants to carry my burdens.

3. God plans for us to live a prosperous life, full of hope. As long as God, Who knows the future, plans your agenda, you can be filled with hope instead of worry and fear. Your responsibility is to make sure you are following His agenda, not yours.

4. When we say "I shall not want," we express confidence—we have no concern for our future. "I do not want" is an expression of past experiences. God does not keep us from having needs, but He can keep us from wanting things we do not need.

5. They are self-willed and rebellious, choosing to wander in a wilderness of fear and worry.

6. Psalm 23:2 pictures a contented sheep. If you were to live out Psalm 100, you would be contented, happy, and worry free. Words of praise and words of worry do not mix.

7. *Let students answer privately.*

8. His joy. This joy is restored when we confess our sin.

9. You must abide in Christ each day. Believers do this by staying in a close relationship with Him each day, drawing upon His strength to keep going. We must dwell on God's promises instead of our problems.

10. A person filled with worry is not trusting God. "But without faith it is impossible to please him" (Hebrews 11:6).

11. When we do not trust God, we are saying to others, "My God is unable to help me."

12. God wants us to walk with a confident trust in Him instead of trying to figure out tomorrow. He wants to guide our steps (Psalm 37:23).

13. We have no peace, and our lives are no longer full of right actions that please God.

14. When you can trust God to be your deliverer and strength, you can

have joy in your heart no matter what. This joy will allow you to rise above your problems, because you know God will take care of you.

15. If you will memorize God's Word, you can think on it instead of on your problems throughout the day. One day you will actually thank God for your problems if they teach you to trust Him. If you find yourself wandering away from God's Word, quickly get back to where you were—memorizing and meditating on God's Word.

16. We will not trust God. Instead, we take matters into our own hands and do things our way instead of God's way.

17. He is a person full of the joy of the Lord. His heart is full of peace and contentment; he has music in his heart and in his home. His love for God overflows on others, and nothing can rob him of this joy, because he believes God surrounds him with His shield of protection.

18. *Ephesians 4:32*—God forgives us when we fail. *Philippians 4:13–19*—He gives us His strength to handle anything He calls upon us to endure. He provides all our needs materially, emotionally, and spiritually. *Isaiah 26:3*—He gives us peace.

19. Even when we are unfaithful, He is always faithful and thinking of our spiritual well-being.

20. *Personal answers; ask for responses.* We may not always treat others right, but God always treats us right. God will let us go only so far in our sin. He will then chasten us to remind us that He still loves us.

21. Confidence in our eternal relationship with God is a matter of trust. Do you believe Christ died, was buried, and rose again to pay for your salvation? Have you confessed with your mouth that you believe Christ died for you, and have you asked Him to save you? If so, John 10:25–29 says that you have eternal life, and there is no end to "eternal." To guarantee the security of our salvation, Christ gave us a beautiful picture in verses 28 and 29. We are in Christ's hand, and God's hand is over His. Nothing can take us out of Their hands. We are secure!

Lesson 6

1. Bitterness, or anything else that could defile us, is sin.
2. No; his or her speech will reveal the bitter spirit.
3. Her brother Amnon raped her.
4. Absalom told her not to tell anyone else. So she retreated to his

house to live a desolate life full of shame, separated from everyone else.

5. He hated Amnon for what he had done, and he had Amnon killed.

6. It is everlasting, or unconditional. God does not love us because we are worthy of His love; He loves us because it is His nature to love (1 John 4:16).

7. God.

8. We can remember that God is just and that He always does what is right.

9. *Ask for responses.* Possible answers include an unpleasant job, chronic pain, financial loss, an unhappy marriage, or an unhappy home situation.

10. A person in a difficult situation could dwell on his difficulty and forget to count all his other blessings.

11. If we are focused on God—His daily benefits to us (Psalm 68:19) and His will for us (40:8)—we will not be bitter; we will be delighted.

12. Bitterness is extremely destructive because it not only destroys the person hanging onto it, but it also hurts everyone else who comes into contact with the bitter person.

13. An unforgiving spirit.

14. The merciful king is like God, Who forgives us. The unmerciful servant is like each of us when we will not forgive others. God forgives us when we do not deserve to be forgiven. He expects us to forgive others who do not deserve to be forgiven.

15. *Have the class take time for self-examination.*

16. Feelings of bitterness, anger, resentment, hatred, guilt. *Have the group members share some of their thoughts.*

17. (a) Bitterness, defile; (b) cleansing; (c) kind, forgiving; (d) Christ; (e) forgive; (f) answered; (g) spiritual; (h) God, pleases, authority.

Lesson 7

1. They become conceited, and they trust in their riches instead of God.

2. He wants us to enjoy them but not to love them more than we love Him.

3. Money itself is not evil, but it can put us in bondage to dis-

contentment, covetousness, greed, and envy.

4. The one you are the most concerned about—God (spiritual) or "mammon" (material)—is the one you love and live for.

5. Discontentment with our belongings may lead to financial bondage. Learning to be content on the income God provides is very difficult for families living in this materialistic age. Most American families live beyond their means.

6. We must recognize we are coveting things we do not need. Contentment must be learned; it will not just happen. However, it starts with seeing the difference between a need and a want.

7. Real living does not revolve around all the material things we have.

8. We are rich toward God when we have what money can't buy—eternal life and a joy-filled, contented, peaceful, and Spirit-controlled life.

9. Believers might forget the Lord, and they might go after other gods, one of them being money.

10. They must put God first in their lives and trust Him to provide for their needs, not their wants.

11. When we freely give for the ministry of Christ, we can expect God to meet our needs.

12. They spend too much! Few families who are content with the basics—food, clothing, and shelter—experience financial pressure.

13. With God's help and a definite plan, you can begin to see the end of your debts.

14. Most of our wants are not needs. We must learn to be content with what God has provided for us and quit always wanting what we cannot afford.

15. *Ask the group members if they did this. Ask if any of them were surprised by what they learned.*

16. Take one-fifth, or 20 percent, of all his crop during the plenteous years and store it away so that there would be sufficient food during the seven years of famine.

17. In your working and productive years, save so that you have sufficient store for your nonproductive years. Saving is for long-term purposes as well as for a multitude of short-term needs.

Lesson 8

1. Forgiveness is the loving, voluntary cancellation of a debt. The debtor goes free. We turn loose all feelings of revenge and resentment.

2. We may not be able to forget, even when we have extended forgiveness. However, we can choose not to remember by not dwelling on the offense or bringing it up again. If we keep bringing it up, we know we have not really forgiven. We still feel that the person needs to pay.

3. What you give, you get. Give love—get back love. Give forgiveness—get back forgiveness.

4. Forgiveness is a must for fellowship with God. An unforgiving spirit keeps our prayers from being answered.

5. As sin.

6. The Lord will not hear our prayers.

7. We become angry; we pout and refuse to do what the Father wants. Then He has to deal with us.

8. Go to that person and try to restore fellowship.

9. Jesus was probably referring to significant offenses, or sins, that are ongoing problems and break down intimacy and trust in a relationship.

10. To confront a person about a problem with the goal of restoring fellowship. Unless rebuke is tied to forgiveness, it is of no value.

11. We must speak in a loving way and with a kind, forgiving spirit.

12. True repentance involves a change of mind and actions. The repentant person must admit being wrong and must do all he or she can to make restitution. When a person is truly repentant, that person will confess his or her wrong and offer no excuse for sin but will humbly plead for mercy and quietly accept the consequences.

13. He confessed he had sinned against God and others (v. 18). He pled for mercy; he acknowledged he deserved nothing. He was willing to work as a hired servant (v. 19).

14. He held nothing against the son. Real love and forgiveness go hand in hand. Forgiving requires that we love; loving requires that we forgive.

15. The father was full of joy and *gladness* (v. 32). The older son was full of *anger* and jealousy (vv. 28–30).

16. We must keep forgiving over and over again, sometimes for the same offense.

17. They felt unsure that they could forgive. They asked Him to increase their faith.

18. We are always ready to accept forgiveness from God and others but often are reluctant in giving it.

19. *Encourage each person to answer these questions.*

Lesson 9

1. I can't do it, I can't win, there is no use trying. The negative "I can't" complex makes people give up before they ever try.

2. *Numbers 13:31*—The enemies' strength. The people were too strong. *Numbers 13:33*—The enemies' size. They exaggerated by calling the sons of Anak giants and themselves grasshoppers.

3. Their past life. They thought they had been better off in bondage in Egypt.

4. Unbelief and rebellion.

5. They were never able to enter the Promised Land, which flowed with milk and honey.

6. *Exodus 13:21*—Cloud and pillar. The Lord led them with a cloud by day and a pillar of fire at night. *Exodus 14:13–16*—Path through the sea. God opened the Red Sea, and they walked through on dry ground. The enemies chasing them were swallowed up in the sea. *Exodus 16:4*—Manna. God rained manna, or bread, from Heaven each day to feed them. *Exodus 17:1–7*—Water out of a rock. When they had no water to drink, God brought water from a rock.

7. An abundant life full of joy.

8. We fail to really believe God and never enter into the abundant life He has planned for us. God often has to chasten us for our unbelief instead of blessing us for our faith.

9. *Have a few group members share their answers.*

10. *Exodus 4:10–12*—Moses. He felt he absolutely could not do what God had asked him to do. As far as he was concerned, it was out of the realm of possibility. *Genesis 17:17*—Abraham. When he was one

hundred years old, and Sarah ninety, God told them that they would have a child. To Abraham, this was absolutely impossible. *Daniel 2:10–16*—Daniel. He knew that only God could give him the ability to interpret the king's dream. *1 Kings 17:8–12*—A widow. God wanted her to feed Elijah. She had enough provisions for only one last meal to feed her son and herself. She wondered how she could possibly make the food stretch any further. *John 6:1–7*—Philip. Jesus told Philip to feed five thousand people. Philip doubted but sincerely asked, "Where can we possibly get enough money to buy food for this multitude?"

11. *Moses*—God provided Aaron, Moses' brother, to speak for him. It is interesting that Moses, who thought he could not speak, gave the great discourses in the book of Deuteronomy. Our inabilities only amplify God's great ability. *Abraham*—Abraham chose to believe God in spite of the impossibility. He stands as a testimony of the power of faith. *Daniel*—Daniel asked his friends to join him in praying to the One Who knows all things. Daniel knew God and understood how to lay hold of God for his needs. *The widow at Zarephath*—She submitted to the word of the prophet. She demonstrated the value of a submissive spirit to the word of God. *Philip*—Philip took what was at hand and gave it to Christ to bless and multiply. Philip found, as we often do, that Christ can take what seems to be totally inadequate and make it sufficient to meet the need.

12. *Ask for responses.*

13. Everything God allows into our lives can enrich us if we receive it by faith instead of resisting it.

14. These are people who use a weakness they have as an excuse for not doing better or for not trying at all. Or a person might develop a limp to have an excuse for not performing as well as others. Without the limp, he would be responsible for his poor performance; but with it, he believes he won't be blamed.

15. *Ask the group members to examine themselves and write down their difficulties.*

16. *Ask for responses.* In our own strength we are powerless to trust God. With God's help and strength to empower us, we can do anything God asks of us. When we exchange our weak, puny strength for His supernatural strength, we no longer have to look at

situations and say, "I just can't trust God."

17. We can share with others how God helped us and what we learned from our experience. We can also remind them that God loves them just as much as He loves us and wants to do the same for them.

Lesson 10

1. The human heart was made with an insatiable longing to be loved.

2. *Isaiah 6:1*—Death. *Deuteronomy 24:3*—Divorce or separation. *Genesis 12:1*—Leaving your homeland to move to a new country or just moving to a new location.

3. Feelings of emptiness and futility.

4. He created male and female so that they could be companions to one another.

5. A need to have fellowship with God and others and have companionship with them.

6. Only God can heal a broken heart, and only He can free people who feel they are imprisoned. God has a cure for every need we have. He has everything we need for life and godliness.

7. Solitude is voluntary. We deliberately choose to withdraw from others. We often need solitude to renew ourselves or to give us creative new energy. Loneliness is involuntary and unwanted. It tends to bring feelings of depression and desolation; it can be destructive.

8. We must be still in God's presence each day to really get to know Him.

9. Times of solitude with God will help us be better prepared to handle life's pressures and to help those around us who are lonely and need our help.

10. He was transformed into a man who had power with God and man.

11. *Have a few people in the group share their experiences and answer the question.*

12. God is sovereign and does as He pleases in our lives. For some He creates peace, and for others He allows calamity. When we

learn to accept God's sovereign control in our lives, we can have peace in the midst of calamity. "In acceptance lieth peace." In times of solitude and peace we have time to think about the greatness and power of our God, Who has everything under control.

13. *Have someone who has experienced a loss share with the group.*

14. Time can make the pain seem less intense and blunt the sharp edge of sorrow, but only God can comfort and heal the brokenhearted.

15. Becoming obsessed with a loss shows a lack of confidence that God has done what was right from His perspective. We do not always understand God's way, but we don't need to understand. We just need to say, "As for God His way is perfect."

16. A brawling wife or husband could be worse than no mate at all.

17. The loss of friendship from relatives of the person's former mate or sometimes the divorced person's own relatives. Also, the friends of the former mate may no longer want the person's friendship.

18. *Have someone who has gone through a divorce express his or her thoughts.*

19. A divorced person must deal with forgiveness. An unforgiving spirit is like a cancer that eats away at the soul. There can be no sense of peace and contentment until we forgive. We cannot overcome loneliness until we experience peace and contentment.

20. God can help them to be content with a new role in life, and He will supply their need for friends if that's what they need to ease the pain of loneliness.

21. Everyone needs a companion or friend.

22. When someone has a friend or companion, he has someone with whom he can share his joys and sorrows.

23. A lonely person must take the first step toward making new friendships.

Lesson 11

1. *Ask the group members to share their ideas.*

2. *Have some people in the group share their ideas on causes of depression.*

3. Women whose system is estrogen deprived can often experience some of the symptoms of depression. Men and women who have an

untreated thyroid problem may experience symptoms of depression.

4. The discouraged still believe that things can change; the depressed are hopeless and feel there is no use in trying anymore.

5. Fatigue.

6. He may have felt dried up spiritually—he was thirsting for God.

7. Those around him were saying, "If God is so good, why doesn't He help you?" David might have even been asking himself the same question.

8. David's comment might picture an empty person.

9. He might have wanted to ask God, "What have I done to deserve this? I've tried to do right."

10. David was rebuking himself, asking, "Why are you depressed? Get focused back on God."

11. In his self-talk, David was facing his problem and identifying the source of his help.

12. David was trying to remember all the good things God had done in the past.

13. This remembering helped him get his focus on God and off himself.

14. He felt overwhelmed, as if he were being tossed around in painful waves of distress and turmoil.

15. David had not lost confidence in God. He kept praying and believing God could help him.

16. His enemies kept chiding him and asking, "Where is your God?" David might have felt as if God had forgotten him and didn't care how much he was hurting. It seemed God just kept letting David's enemies slap David in the face with their ridicule and their hurtful remarks.

17. His countenance needed healing—he needed to quit looking so downcast and sad. He needed a smile on his face again. He was confident he would be praising God again with a cheerful heart and face.

18. These sixteen verses contain fifty-two personal pronouns referring to David.

19. David was focused more on himself than on God.

20. Forty-two.

21. His eyes were still on God; he had not turned his back on

God, but he was focused more on himself.

22. Self-pity.

Lesson 12

1. *1 Peter 2:2*—Believers have a desire to read God's Word so that they can grow spiritually. *Psalm 119:105*—The Word of God is a guide for believers' lives. *John 14:15*—Christians want to obey God's commands. *Romans 8:14–16*—The Holy Spirit dwells in believers. *1 John 4:7, 8*—Believers love the people of God. *Matthew 6:14, 15*—Christians have a forgiving spirit. *2 Corinthians 5:17*—Believers' lives are changing.

2. *Ask the group members to think on this question. Ask if anyone received Christ as Savior during this study.*

3. Find pleasure in reading and obeying the Word.

4. By reading and meditating on it. A casual glimpse does not enrich the soul enough to bring great delight and joy to the life.

5. Strong—"like a tree"; productive—brings forth fruit; persevering—does "not wither"; prosperous—"whatsoever he doeth shall prosper."

6. Christ is the source of our strength. His Spirit is like a river of water running through our emotions, mind, will, and bodies.

7. The fruit of the Spirit: love, joy, peace, longsuffering, gentleness, goodness, faithfulness, meekness, and self-control.

8. The happy Christian brings forth the fruit of longsuffering when patience is needed to endure, peace in the times of trials, meekness when submission is needed, and self-control when "no" is needed.

9. He has a quiet determination and consistency.

10. His or her prosperity is inward, not necessarily outward. Contentment is a way of life for this happy person. He or she is rich! Who could buy love, joy, peace, and all the other fruit of the Spirit?

11. It starts with a personal relationship with Jesus that gives a person eternal life. This relationship is maintained and grows as the person daily reads, meditates on, and obeys the Word of God.

12. Going through a daily routine of reading without the thought of building a closer relationship with Jesus Christ.

13. *Have a few people share their methods for daily Bible reading.*